THE Wisdom
OF DR. LOW

Words to Live By

All quotations are from the following works of neuropsychiatrist Abraham Low MD, compiled with the permission of Phyllis Low Berning and Marilyn Low Schmitt:

Mental Health Through Will Training
(Glencoe IL, Willett Publishing Co., 3rd edition, 1997; © Phyllis Low Berning and Marilyn Low Schmitt, 1997; first published 1950)

Peace Versus Power in the Family
(Glencoe IL, Willett Publishing Co., 2nd edition, 1967; © Phyllis Low Berning and Marilyn Low Schmitt; first published 1943)

Manage Your Fears, Manage Your Anger
(Glencoe IL, Willett Publishing Co., 1995; © Phyllis Low Berning and Marilyn Low Schmitt, 1995; lectures presented in 1953 and 1954)

Selections from Dr. Low's Works (1950-1953)
(Copyright ©1966 Mae Low © 2005 Recovery International under terms of a license agreement with the copyright holder executed on October 11, 1966.

Also, by Neil and Margaret Rau:
My Dear Ones
(Chicago, Recovery Inc. reprint, 1986; © Neil and Margaret Rau, 1971)

© *Recovery International*

CONTENTS

BOOK ABBREVIATIONS

By Abraham Low, MD:

MHTWT = Mental Health Through Will Training (Glencoe IL, Willett Publishing Co., 3rd edition, 1997; © Phyllis Low Berning and Marilyn Low Schmitt, 1997; first published 1950)

MFMA = Manage Your Fears, Manage Your Anger (Glencoe IL, Willett Publishing Co., 1995; © Phyllis Low Berning and Marilyn Low Schmitt, 1995; lectures presented in 1953 and 1954)

P v. P = Peace Versus Power in the Family (Glencoe IL, Willett Publishing Co., 2nd edition, 1967; © Phyllis Low Berning and Marilyn Low Schmitt; first published 1943)

Selections = Selections from Dr. Low's Works (1950-1953) (Copyright ©1966 Mae Low © 2005 Recovery International under terms of a license agreement with the copyright holder executed on October 11, 1966.

By Neil and Margaret Rau:

MDO = My Dear Ones (Chicago, Recovery Inc. reprint, 1986; © Neil and Margaret Rau, 1971)

INTRODUCTION

Welcome to the Wisdom of Dr. Low. In the following pages, you will be able to focus on what Dr. Low had to say about a myriad of subjects, including intimate personal reflections. By studying Dr. Low's teaching in this way, you can potentially gain a deeper grasp of the principles, ideas and techniques that are central to the comprehensive system of self-help that he developed. A note of caution, however: the books that these quotes are taken from hold a richness and depth that these excerpts can only hint at, therefore, direct study of Dr. Low's writings is highly recommended. One way to explore that "richness" is to use the pages cited for the quotes as a pathway back into the texts in order to get a broader contextual understanding of what the quotes mean. Since there is some overlap among the topics listed, you will occasionally see the same quote under different headings. Dr. Low's ability to explore several ideas in the course of a few sentences also led to the need for repetition. We hope that your exploration into the writings of this cognitive-behavioral pioneer brings you a new level of inner peace, greater self-awareness and a revitalization of your mental and emotional health.

Thank you to all who have kept the Wisdom of Dr. Low alive in our communities through our weekly Recovery International Meetings.

A special thank you to Cliff Brown whose effort in compiling these Wisdoms made this volume possible.

WISDOM OF DR. LOW BY TOPICS

ANGER

"Understanding is the *will to understand* but temperamental persons are impelled by the *will to misunderstand*. The misunderstandings furnish them the reasons and excuses for practicing their temper. The classical example is the husband who goes into a rage because dinner is not ready the moment he enters the home. If this enraged husband had the will to understand he would not have to dig deep to find the reason for the delay. He would easily understand, without effort of thought or special inquiry, that domestic affairs are never expected to run to schedule." (P v. P, p. 193)

"My patients claim they suffer from frightening sensations, overpowering impulses, torturing thoughts and devitalized feelings. But I tell them that this is a half-truth at best; that what they actually suffer from is—their philosophy. And if their philosophy is based on the assumption that in their spells and tantrums their feelings are real and their thoughts are right, well, that is precisely the philosophy of temper. In the ordinary burst of temper, whether it be presymptomatic or postsymptomatic, you *feel* the insult or injury was a 'real' outrage, and *think* you are 'right' in considering it a deliberate hurt." (MHTWT, p. 75)

"If you want to get rid of your nervous symptoms, you must establish, or re-establish, relaxation. You can call it peace. You can call it equilibrium. You can call it adjustment, but, essentially, it is relaxation. And if somebody wants to restore relaxation or acquire relaxation, he has to do one thing and that is to banish fear and anger from his system as much as can be done." (MFMA, p. 222)

"Your fear and anger reactions-this means your temperamental reactions-originally do not want to be controlled. They want to express themselves. In fear, you want to run. In anger, you want to strike out. You want to express your anger in an action, this means in an aggressive action. You want to express your fear in an action, that means in a defensive reaction." (MFMA, p. 230)

"If you declare something ridiculous-your own reaction-if you declare it as ridiculous, then you don't take it seriously. And there is never an anger that is not taken seriously." (MFMA, p. 293)

ATTITUDE

"What is of importance is not the event but the attitude that you take to the event…The attitude is yours…and…can be controlled, can be changed, can be improved…The event usually cannot." (MFMA, p. 108)

"I want you to distinguish clearly and energetically between the event that happens in environment, either in outer environment or in inner environment, and the attitude which you take-not the event, but you. The attitude is yours. It is not of the event. And if you bungle, it's due to your attitude, and the attitude can be controlled, can be changed, can be improved. It can be omitted, it can be adopted, it can be manipulated. The event usually cannot." (MFMA, p. 108)

AVERAGENESS

"When I think of myself as average, then everything that is average, that is done by people on an average, is permissible and I will not blame myself for doing it." (MFMA, p. 73)

"Be certain that average persons develop extreme reactions in some field of life." (MFMA, p. 20)

" [My patients] shy away, persistently and doggedly, from the total view that their symptoms are of the average variety although more persistent in duration and more resistant to management." (MHTWT, p. 212-213)

"Stop blaming yourself for your averageness, for your average human imperfection, for human limitations. And if you stop blaming yourself, you will, incidentally, naturally whittle down that thing that you now call, that I ask you to call *the passion for self-distrust.*" (MFMA, p. 311)

"When my patients begin to lash out against themselves, to accuse themselves, to condemn themselves, they do something that gives the self-condemnation duration…they think of how they acted previously…When I look back into my past, I could easily exclaim, 'Oh, what a rascal have I been!' Well, what of it? So, I have been a rascal numerous times… I am an average person. I am like everybody is." (MFMA, p. 42-43)

"I make…mistakes, too, …and then I ask myself, 'what's the matter with me?' And my answer is, 'Well, nothing is the matter with me. I am average.' And that's what average people do." (MFMA, p. 98-99)

"Nervousness and nervous symptoms are universal and average and…to get well means to become again an average nervous person who experiences nervous reactions in many phases of his life but has implicit confidence in the trustworthiness of his basic functions." (Selections, p. 10)

"In Recovery, the patient is made to realize the fallacy of the romanticist estimate that life is either supreme bliss or dreary desolation. He learns that there is a middle ground of solid averageness in which the tonic quality of realistic action does away with the hectic hunt for picnics which have a sorry way of turning into panics." (Selections, p. 52)

"In my more than thirty years of intensive experience with patients I have met nothing but average cases. In all of them I have observed the following pattern: There are the average run of symptoms which are due to average type of tenseness, and the tenseness is created or maintained by either temper or self-diagnosing or by both. And the average patient can easily discover within himself both temper and self-diagnosing." (Selections, p. 109)

"To admit one's limitations is humility, to insist on one's superior knowledge is vanity." (MHTWT, p. 163)

"Everybody, not only my patients, has the natural impulse to prove the superiority of his thinking abilities (intellectual validity) and to demonstrate the exquisite quality of his strength, forcefulness and prowess (romantic vitality)." (MHTWT, p. 163-164)

"Do your best, your average best, not to be careless, but only your average best. I will add, your average should be good average. You should live a life as the desirable people in the community appear to live their lives. Whether they do it, I can't tell you." (MFMA, p. 74)

"If you adopt ideals, and be sure you all have adopted the ideals that every good average person has adopted, then march towards the ideal. Don't think that you must reach it...That's not the purpose of life: to reach the ideal. At any rate, I don't think it is. The purpose of life is to come as close to the ideal as you can manage, but remember humans have limitations. I have yet to see a human being that is a saint. I have yet to see a human being that is sinless. The ideal would demand that you are sinless. I have as yet to see a human being that is faultless, and if I saw one, I wouldn't want to associate with him. I wouldn't want any of my children to become faultless. They should have their average faults. That makes them human." (MFMA, p. 74-75)

"The average person has fears, and headaches, and numbness, and develops a palpitation here and a pressure there, but if he feels average, then he takes it for granted that that is coming to him and therefore doesn't work himself up over it. If he feels average, he will not blame himself for having palpitations, not even for having the feeling that he is dying away. He will simply take it for granted that he is an average human being with the average human limitations." (MFMA, p. 75)

"And if anybody wants to look down his nose on Recovery and say, 'Look here, they talk trivialities,' then I'll agree with him. We talk trivialities, and it is these trivialities which touch on averageness, and it is the principle of averageness that makes you human and healthy. And I will advise you, don't expect that your condition, being as complex as it is – and I don't deny that – requires complex methods to check it and to conquer it. That's not so. The simple method is always the superior procedure." (MFMA, p. 76)

"There are very few people who do not think of themselves as being of a superior breed, as ranking above the 'common herd,' that is, as being exceptional. With most of them it is merely a dream, an ambition and aspiration. They hope to be exceptional but know they are 'nothing but average.' In their dreams and fancies they are romanto-intellectuals but in actual practice they behave as realists. Their sense of exceptionality is properly controlled by their knowledge of being average." (MHTWT, p. 248)

"Most if not all people embrace both the philosophy of exceptionality and that of averageness. The average person adjusts and balances the two philosophies in such a manner that the one (averageness) is leading and controlling, the other (exceptionality) is led and controlled. If this is done, then decisions and actions are balanced and adjusted on a practical level while dreams and fancies are given free play on an imaginative level." (MHTWT, p. 248)

"I remember many of the evil things I have done, not all. What do I do then? Why do I not sink in the ground with shame? It was an average past. Why should I blame myself for an average past?" (MDO, p. 144)

"But look what goes on in me. What a wretched person I am. I have worked for many years and heaven knows how many mistakes I make when I work. I make a great many mistakes…I know about black spots in my life. Nobody else knows about them. I could work myself up about the dusky part. It all comes to this matter: averageness. Everybody is average." (MDO, p. 144)

"If somebody should hate any other person, in-law or not, because that person has been very unfriendly to the one who now hates him, I would not consider this a verdict on the character or the personality of that hating person. I will not approve of it, but I will say this is an average reaction." (MFMA, p. 84)

"Do you understand now that having a good sense of humor and feeling average are the same thing? And looking on his troubles with a great sense of importance is the same thing as having no sense of humor. So, this matter of importance is opposed to the matter of averageness, and the sense of humor is opposed, naturally, to the sense of importance." (MFMA, p. 99)

"Everybody who has a head pressure-I have them frequently-does not immediately go into tantrums because it is unbearable. The average person bears a pain, but the patient does not want to... The average person bears a pain, especially a pain that he has had repeatedly in the past, because he is linked to the past and does not particularly consider this day but the total time of his total life. And looking back into his previous life, into this total of his life, he knows that his head pressure has been severe at many times in his history, and it hasn't killed him, and he bore it bravely and patiently, so he bears it again. He is determined to bear it again." (MFMA, p. 104-105)

"For anybody to want to be average means to give up the hope of being superior. And people don't like that. They have lived - relatively speaking, the one twenty years and the other thirty and the other sixty - and they have spent their lifetime in dreaming to accomplish greatness. It doesn't have to be the greatness of a presidency of the United States, but to accomplish something exceptional in their group at least, not in humanity. And now they should give up this sixty –year habit. That's a big bill to fill. That's a big order. But here in Recovery you must accept this big order and carry it out." (MFMA, p. 155)

"I have yet to know a person that can tolerate continuous stimulation-or, more so, irritation, but even stimulation-if it is continuous. Let just a hum go on in your home. That can't do you any harm. But if it goes on for half hours and hours, then it exasperates you. You want to get rid of this hum. And yet the hums don't criticize you, [don't] start an argument with you, but the very fact that there is endless repetition antagonizes everybody." (MFMA, p. 168)

"This phenomenon of somebody changing abruptly from one state to the opposite state, from liveliness to dullness, from sympathy to even hatred, from love to hatred, all of this is nothing uncommon. And I mention very, very spectacular contrasts: for instance the change from love to hatred, and that even is not at all uncommon. It's, indeed, I think, frequent. If this is true, then why should one be amazed at that?" (MFMA, p. 277)

"I cannot imagine any human being that would be satisfied with his existence, with his work, with his conduct, with his accomplishments. If he were, he would be a remarkable person. It is simply not human to be satisfied most of the time. Naturally, nobody can ever be satisfied all the time, but it is extremely difficult to be satisfied most of the time, or a great length of time." (MFMA, p. 46)

"If you don't face your frustrations, your palpitations, your pressures, your numbnesses, your depressions, your fatigue as average events, if you believe they are emergencies, then, of course, you'll get dismal ideas into your head. How long can you stand a life that is full of emergencies?" (MFMA, p. 48)

BALANCE

"Whenever you reach the point where most of your actions are controlled and only part of your actions are easily expressed, then you have balance…and that is that kind of balance in which the group reactions predominate over the individualistic reactions, and that's the only kind of balance we want in life: the balance in which control predominates over reckless expression." (MFMA, p. 231)

"In inner life, nothing should be equal. If you have an equal amount of honesty as you have of dishonesty, that's no balance. Be sure that's no balance. If you have just as much good control as you have temper, that's no balance. You see, in life we don't want equality, a balance that means equality. We want a preponderance of control over life expression." (MFMA, p. 231)

BELIEFS

"The bulk of the suffering which is the lot of my patients does not stem from their 'dreadful' experiences but rather from their frightening beliefs." (Selections, p. 62)

"If the brain is to conceive fear ideas, they must come to the brain. Seldom will the brain develop these fear ideas out of thin air... The brain must get the impression that there is a situation that connotes danger. But the brain, confronted with an impression of this kind, must accept the impression. It can reject it. Anybody can, with his brain, refuse to believe." (MFMA, p. 348)

"When you claim that your feelings are hurt, what you actually mean is that some cherished belief of yours has been doubted, questioned, ignored, rejected or, worse yet, ridiculed, treated with irony, not taken seriously...hurt feelings...is a misnomer for beliefs not shared." (Selections, p. 20-21)

"Nobody loses his temper unless he is or feels he is wronged or insulted intentionally." (MHTWT, p. 392)

"With us in Recovery it is an axiom that while a nervous ailment is not necessarily caused by distorted beliefs, nevertheless, if it persists beyond a reasonable time, its continuance, stubbornness and 'resistance' are produced by continuing, stubborn and resisting' beliefs." (Selections, p. 70)

"Strange as it may sound, the philosophy of Recovery is based unqualifiedly and unreservedly on this matter of belief. All its techniques have for their aim the intention to plant in the patient's mind the correct beliefs (about nervous health) offered by the physician and to purge it of the false beliefs held by himself." (Selections, p. 69)

"My patients claim they suffer from frightening sensations, overpowering impulses, torturing thoughts and devitalized feelings. But I tell them that this is a half-truth at best; that what they actually suffer from is—their philosophy. And if their philosophy is based on the assumption that in their spells and tantrums their feelings are real and their thoughts are right, well, that is precisely the philosophy of temper. In the ordinary burst of temper, whether it be presymptomatic or postsymptomatic, you *feel* the insult or injury was a 'real' outrage, and *think* you are 'right' in considering it a deliberate hurt." (MHTWT, p. 75)

"You will agree that if you fear something you think of that something as a danger. You will also admit that in order to fear a danger you must believe it is real and not imaginary. In other words, you must take the danger seriously and be convinced of its reality. All you have to do to dispose of a fear is to refuse to believe that there is danger. Then you will ignore it or laugh it out of existence. If you laugh at a thing and ridicule it you cannot possibly fear it. That is the reason why a sense of humor is such a strong antidote against fear." (MHTWT, p. 362)

"The difference between a person that gets easily rattled or scared and a person that is calm is essentially the philosophy which the persons have. I will add, the philosophy that anybody has is either one that is pessimistic, more or less pessimistic about human nature, or one that is more or less optimistic. And you can't have an optimistic philosophy if you think that you have to follow extreme, exceptional, and singular standards." (MFMA, p. 74)

"I have concluded [that] if the patient refuses to drop a belief, then he must have conceived of that belief as a value, and a high value." (MFMA, p. 49)

"I doubt whether I ever heard anybody or saw anybody write a sentence in a book that fear is a belief. I doubt it. At any rate, if it has been done, it happened so seldom that I don't remember having read it. And when it came to me once, well, I can't get my patients rid of fear. How can I do that except over years and years of analysis-you know, that's usually the method-then I began to search for some method that is simpler. And it took me time to find out this trivial truth: that, after all, fear is a belief, the belief that there is danger. Now I knew what to do about fear. If it's a belief, well, then I can train the patient to do what I do every few minutes, certainly every few hours." (MFMA, 267)

"I accept beliefs, and then I drop them, then I pick them up again. Everybody can do that. I wait for somebody, then it comes to me, well, there he is, so I believe he's coming. Then I look, I see it isn't he, so I drop the belief. And then I begin to think of him, that he may be out of town. Then I get the belief that I am in danger, that I will not find him. Then I begin to think about it and realize, well, he couldn't be out of town because I just saw him this morning or spoke to him over the phone. Now I change the belief that the man is out of town, and I pick up the belief that he is in town. And these are in important situations where I am eager to meet somebody. These are not even trivialities. They may be important situations. And in such important situations, you drop beliefs , you pick them up, you retain them, you don't, or you try to get rid of them. Beliefs can be manipulated." (MFMA, p. 267-268)

"I didn't know how to manipulate fears. And I still don't know except if I make the patient change his beliefs. And so I must give him my beliefs, and I must form my beliefs first. And so…I formed the belief that the patient suffered from beliefs, from the belief of danger, or, in angry temper, from the belief that somebody did him wrong." (MFMA, p. 268)

"It's a simple method. You just tell somebody to drop his belief, and he could do it. It's simple, but he doesn't drop it. He keeps his belief. And if I want the patient to drop beliefs, well, he makes an effort, but they don't work. They certainly don't work immediately. And there was one thing that I forgot about…when I formulated this theory: I forgot the fact that humans develop habits, and habits are stubborn." (MFMA, p. 268)

"My patients have an extraordinary talent for working themselves up and for self-diagnosing. And so they are always living in that dreadful psychology, which means that their life is full of danger, of the dangers of emergencies. I, for one, cannot imagine a more dreadful sort of life. And you know how dreadful your life has been, and sometimes still is. So why don't you do something? What I ask you to do is to change your beliefs, the belief that your life is steeped in emergencies, in extreme danger, and everybody can either accept a belief or refuse to believe." (MFMA, p. 49)

DANGER

"The best means of reducing an idea of danger to its absurdity is to act against it." (MHTWT, p. 366-367)

"If the brain is to conceive fear ideas, they must come to the brain. Seldom will the brain develop these fear ideas out of thin air… The brain must get the impression that there is a situation that connotes danger. But the brain, confronted with an impression of this kind, must accept the impression. It can reject it. Anybody can, with his brain, refuse to believe." (MFMA, p. 348)

"All you have to do to dispose of a fear is to refuse to believe that there is danger. Then you will ignore it or laugh it out of existence. If you laugh at a thing and ridicule it you cannot possibly fear it. That is the reason why a sense of humor is such a strong antidote against fear." (MHTWT, p. 362)

"Such phrases as 'I have to,' 'I can't,' or 'I try my best but can I help it if I don't succeed?' mean that the patient diagnoses his condition as a physical disease in which Fate has paralyzed his Will. No matter how skillfully fitting is the context in which phrases of this kind are used, they mean nothing less than the diagnosis of an organic ailment…the patient refuses to accept the physician's diagnosis of a distressing but harmless nervous disturbance insisting on self-diagnosing it as a serious organic ailment. The tragedy is that self-diagnosing is anything but an innocent pastime. It breeds defeatism and fatalism, continued tenseness and endless agony." (Selections, p. 61)

"The patient does not want to be convinced that his symptoms are harmless. His convictions tend the opposite way. What he wants to see and believe is the emergency nature of his condition, not its harmlessness. The element of emergency he spotlights, the element of harmlessness he blindspots." (Selections, p. 127)

"You can throw off any nervous symptom at any time for a

few seconds or minutes if you spot them as distressing but not dangerous. The symptom will come back in the next minute or so. But you can get rid of it again for a short while, and then again and again and before long you will be rid of the trouble for hours or for days. The symptom will return and keep returning but in the end you will bring it under control by plugging away at it." (MHTWT, p. 139)

"Nervous symptoms are the result of tenseness and if you 'spot them as distressing but not dangerous' you dismiss the idea of danger; and without the thought of danger in your brain you feel safe; and if you feel safe you relax; and if you relax you lose your tenseness; and with tenseness gone the symptom disappears. What can be more simple, what more easy to believe and more thoroughly in accord with sense?" (MHTWT, p. 140)

"You will agree that if you fear something you think of that something as a danger. You will also admit that in order to fear a danger you must believe it is real and not imaginary. In other words, you must take the danger seriously and be convinced of its reality. All you have to do to dispose of a fear is to refuse to believe that there is danger. Then you will ignore it or laugh it out of existence. If you laugh at a thing and ridicule it you cannot possibly fear it. That is the reason why a sense of humor is such a strong antidote against fear." (MHTWT, p. 362)

"Worry may be very useful because if I worry in a real danger, in a realistic danger, well, then I'll take the necessary precautions, and a fear of this kind is useful. Even if a fear turns into a scare, it may still be useful, and frequently is. Suppose I have neglected my work, and then something happens that gives me a shock. I get scared. That scare is useful. It will presumably make me pay more attention to my work. But when the patient is given to fear, there is nothing useful about it. He fears all the time. He develops the habit of fearing. Now, look here: Fear, or distrust, or suspicion, should naturally arise only when there is a danger. And I have yet to see the average person that is always in danger for weeks, and months, and years. Yet my patients, once they conceive a fear, are fearful all the time." (MFMA, p. 7)

"If anybody, any one of you, has the infantile idea that you just can manage to hear that there is no danger, and then you think you understand it, and therefore it will be settled in your brain, well, that is wish thinking. I hear plenty of things, and I understand them, and then I go ahead and still practice the habits that I have acquired, although I know now that they are not of the best. That happens to everybody because everybody has harmful habits." (MFMA, p. 9)

"Sensations and feelings rise and fall provided you do not attach the idea of danger at the moment the curve reaches its peak." (MHTWT, p. 356)

"Fear can be remedied only by the certain knowledge that no danger threatens. You cannot gain this knowledge from your own experience which is amateurish and limited to the acquaintance with one single case. What must guide you is my authoritative knowledge which is based on solid study and expert observation. This alone can give you the conviction that no danger whatever attends a night spent in bed even if you feel you 'haven't slept a wink.' " (MHTWT, p. 357)

"How are you going to acquire this knowledge that there is no danger?…Briefly, I'll tell you, such a certain knowledge can only be acquired if you practice it and listen to it and think about it continually till it is settled." (MFMA, p. 9)

"You heard Vicky, who sat to my right here, telling you about her condition. And let me tell you that this condition-the feeling that somebody is dying away-is about the most agonizing thing that I have ever heard about. And be sure I have heard of a multitude of agonies…So Vicky is suffering from a most frightful condition and has only had some relief the past few days. And there she sits here, and did you notice any sign of suffering in her features? Did you notice any trembling of her voice, any strain in her cheeks or in her total carriage? If this can happen, if a condition of such frightfulness can suddenly disappear without leaving a trace behind,

23

how can such a condition be dangerous? I hope you will ponder this question. And we deal here with a most severe condition." (MFMA, p. 119)

"A dog jumps at you, and you get scared...you formed the belief that there is danger. Then you looked at the dog, and you formed the belief there is no danger. The first belief, that there was danger, made you tense. The second belief, there is no danger, removed the tenseness. It wasn't done by the dog. The dog couldn't have removed the tenseness. The dog removed himself, but not the tenseness. And this simple example will show you what we mean by spotting." (MFMA, p. 266)

"I doubt whether I ever heard anybody or saw anybody write a sentence in a book that fear is a belief. I doubt it. At any rate, if it has been done, it happened so seldom that I don't remember having read it. And when it came to me once, well, I can't get my patients rid of fear. How can I do that except over years and years of analysis-you know, that's usually the method-then I began to search for some method that is simpler. And it took me time to find out this trivial truth: that, after all, fear is a belief, the belief that there is danger. Now I knew what to do about fear. If it's a belief, well, then I can train the patient to do what I do every few minutes, certainly every few hours." (MFMA, p. 267)

"There has never been a human being living that-I mean a human, a patient, a human being that is a nervous patient-who would not lose his symptoms instantly, if he actually accepted this dictum that there is no danger, there is only distress." (MFMA, p. 287)

"Anybody who has really accepted that there is no danger gets relief when he first applies this dictum for a few seconds. Then the symptom comes back. If then the patient goes on undeterred to apply the dictum again, the next time when he relaxes, he will relax for five seconds, for seven seconds. The next time he will relax for two minutes; the next time, for an ever-lengthening interval. And I have seen patients getting well quickly because they applied this dictum with determination." (MFMA, p. 288)

"My patients have an extraordinary talent for working themselves up and for self-diagnosing. And so they are always living in that dreadful psychology, which means that their life is full of danger, of the dangers of emergencies. I, for one, cannot imagine a more dreadful sort of life. And you know how dreadful your life has been, and sometimes still is. So why don't you do something? What I ask you to do is to change your beliefs, the belief that your life is steeped in emergencies, in extreme danger, and everybody can either accept a belief or refuse to believe." (MFMA, p. 49)

DEPRESSION

"Patients who suffer from a depression think that whatever they do is wrong. They think whatever they have done in the past is wrong, and they recount past misdemeanors and so-called delinquencies, which have perhaps some basis in fact but are monstrously exaggerated. And you understand that such patients categorically deny that there is anything right in their thinking." (MFMA, p. 66)

"I will advise you, don't go on constantly discouraging yourselves by thinking that your vitality is gone and dead. It is merely dormant. It hibernates. It is not active. And now you can activate it or reactivate it [if you stop maintaining] the idea that anything in your body is dead. Nature works differently. There is nothing dead in the body if you are alive. The only things that are half dead are such structures as hair and nails, but everything else is alive. But it may be dormant, it may be asleep, inactive." (MFMA, p. 68)

"Many things in a nervous patient are depressed and crowded out of the stream of life. They are in life but don't 'stream.' And in order to make the stream flow again, the stream of feeling, the stream of interest, the stream of mental reaction and emotional reaction, what is required is for the patient not to discourage himself. And in order not to discourage himself, the patient must be trained, trained to develop courage, trained to develop the capacity for braving discomfort-even if you call it torture, but it's still discomfort. And once you learn that, after due training, there is no difficulty to have both validity and vitality restored to its former function, which is then as lively as it ever was." (MFMA, p. 68-69)

DOCTOR LOW ON HIMSELF

[Dr. Low speaking about himself] "I am human. Didn't you know that? I hope you do. And as a human being, be sure I share all your imbecilities and your stupidities, and I'm just as dumb as you are in many things, and everybody is. But I take my smartness and my dumbness not too seriously." (MFMA, p. 98)

"I make...mistakes, too, ...and then I ask myself, 'what's the matter with me?' And my answer is, 'Well, nothing is the matter with me. I am average.' And that's what average people do." (MFMA, p. 98-99)

"There are so many things I do not understand that it would be physically impossible to catalogue them. I do not understand why, on some morning I arise and find myself devoid of my customary energy, or why on some occasions I am sprightly and mentally alert and on other occasions my spirit seems to have gone from me and my disposition reaches a low ebb of dullness and indolence that is truly appalling. And I do not understand at all why if I have some unfathomable difficulty it lasts five minutes the one day and two or three hours the other. All of this is beyond my comprehension. Fortunately, it is immaterial whether a nervous condition is or is not understood. What counts is the knowledge that every nervous symptom, no matter how mysterious and incomprehensible, can be controlled through spotting thoughts and commanding muscles. You see, no matter what subject you patients will bring up, my answer is invariably and monotonously: Spot your thoughts and command your muscles!" (Selections, p. 115-116)

"Even with me who has delivered over 1,500 addresses before Recovery gatherings (twice weekly for fifteen years) there is still some fearful anticipation before each speech and a good deal of unfavorable self-critique afterwards...It is human nature to want superior performance and the perfect achievement…And unless you manage to be saint, angel and wizard combined, you will never succeed in getting rid of your nature. Nature cannot be expelled, but in Recovery we have learned that nature can be controlled." (Selections, p. 124)

"I doubt whether ten minutes have ever passed in my adult life in which I have not worried…But if I begin to worry, for instance, about a patient-and that, of course, happens very often to me-then the question is, will I let the worry where it stands by dint of its nature, or will I work it up and process it? Will I process it into an anxiety, into a state of despondency, into a state of great apprehensiveness? Will I develop the feeling of being trapped and hopeless? And that's what we call *processing*. You work yourself up either about a feeling that has arisen, the feeling of fear or anger, or about a symptom." (MFMA, p. 364)

"My daily life is crowded with occasions in which I fumble and falter. While walking on the street I sometimes stumble or bump into another person. Occasionally I slip or fall on the wet or icy sidewalk. At times I actually hurt myself. Nevertheless, I do not conceive a violent distrust of my Self but consider the misstep or mishap as part of my life. The same holds true for numerous other experiences of my daily round. It happens frequently that I talk to people and fear I said too much. Or, I feel I did not say enough or said the wrong thing. Or, I fall into the trap of a slick salesman who, taking advantage of my preoccupation, tricks me into an ill-considered purchase. In all these instances my Self, physical or social, fails me but I do not lose trust in it." (MHTWT, p. 242)

"I have an egregious sense of importance…it always comes up. I always feel, 'I am the smartest, the finest, the most vital person there is,' but I don't believe it." (MDO, p. 143)

"Sometimes I lie down and daydream and then I have all kinds of fantasies how important I will be some day. Well, it will be about time if it should materialize. I'm not just getting younger, you know. And then all of a sudden after a minute or two I remind myself, 'Well, that's all nonsense, why should I dream about greatness and glamour and fame and fortune and so forth?' and then I stop because it appears ridiculous to me. I have applied a sense of humor." (MDO, p. 143-144)

"I remember many of the evil things I have done, not all. What do I do then? Why do I not sink in the ground with shame? It was an average past. Why should I blame myself for an average past?" (MDO, p. 144)

"But look what goes on in me. What a wretched person I am. I have worked for many years and heaven knows how many mistakes I make when I work. I make a great many mistakes…I know about black spots in my life. Nobody else knows about them. I could work myself up about the dusky part. It all comes to this matter: averageness. Everybody is average." (MDO, p. 144)

"I [have] felt insecure but did not become discouraged. I do not say life is not worth living any more. I keep up my courage. I have air hunger frequently. I have frequently awakened at night with pain." (MDO, p. 144)

"Everybody develops habits. When I was a boy, I was awful. I was a nail biter. I bit my nails. That went on for years and years. What did I get out of it? Nothing. Nothing but annoyance, embarrassment, a sense of shame! Tremendous incentive to stop it! It looked ugly. Could I make up my mind to stop it and it stopped? It took years and years. It was a habit." (MDO, p. 144)

"I remember once I went to a physician when I was a youngster, and I told him I sweated at night. I told him I felt palpitations. I told him I felt feverish, and I felt fatigued, tired all the time. Maybe I told him I thought I had tuberculosis. I was pretty dumb and, of course, the great trouble was I must have read an article about it." (MDO, p. 144)

"It [the impulse] always comes by Fate. I get such impulses, much more dreadful impulses. But my nerves have been steeled and trained to develop resistance, and when dreadful and mischievous and lascivious and blasphemous impulses reach my brain, I look away and wait and they will depart. And they depart in no time because my resistance has been strengthened and Fate is not strong enough to break my resistance once it is strengthened through training." (MDO, p. 144)

"Presumably, I have less vanity today than I had a year ago. Presumably, a year ago I had less vanity than I had ten years ago. And go back onto that scale, back to where I was twenty years, and to my teenage period, and be sure I had to whittle down a mountain of vanity to the present state. And there is still a good hill of it left." (MFMA, p. 156)

"If a youngster tells an experienced, elderly person the truth, then that youngster obviously thinks he knows the truth. And that's an awfully difficult task, to know the truth. There are many truths that I struggle with, and I am no longer a youngster, I will assure you. And I still struggle with endless truths and I don't find them. It's an extremely difficult task to know what is the truth and what is not." (MFMA, p. 162-163)

"Spotting is so intricate, so complex that it requires continuous training. Continuous. I mean it. And I tell you how continuous it must be and must be done. I have stumbled on this subject of spotting about fifteen years ago. And in the meantime, I have made it a life task to study this subject. And I tell you I have studied it very perseveringly, day after day, I must say hour after hour, in all these fifteen years. And you should think that now I am a master of spotting. But I am not yet. And whether I will ever be, I don't know. I'm still too slow in finding meanings underneath statements and reactions, far too slow to suit me, although you may be certain that I am much faster than anyone is who has not studied and learned the technique." (MFMA, p. 207)

"The self protrudes itself into every situation. And in that situation in which I find myself so frequently every day, and sometimes almost all day, that I am confronted with a patient or with a group of patients, you may think that in my mind there is then practically nothing than the patient's interest, the patient's concerns, and not my self-concern. But that is not so. I have something that we call self-importance, the sense of self-importance." (MFMA, p. 252)

"I doubt whether five minutes pass in my life when I don't develop angry temper, because I have yet to see the five minutes of my busy life when I don't have irritations, either at home from the children or in my office." (MFMA, p. 291)

"I have frustrations perhaps every minute of my life. For instance, I am, like other people, practically never satisfied with what I am doing. I always feel I could have done better. You wouldn't believe it, perhaps, but I assure you that this is the case." (MFMA, p. 46)

DOMINATION

"What we call *possessive mothers* are certainly mothers that love their children. They would want to take care of their daughter, not of strangers. But along with this love goes this desire to possess the body and the soul, and every act, and every decision of that daughter. And I have seen mothers who don't let their daughters even boil two eggs. They immediately rush up and say, 'Let me do it.' You can't tell me that this is love." (MFMA, p. 80)

"If a father loves his children and constantly teases them so that they really become distracted, or he constantly says *no* when they ask for something, don't tell me that is love. That father may still love the children, but his love is outstripped by something that we call *domination*. He has no respect for the desires of the children. The children have no desire to constantly [be] teased. They have certainly no desire to be constantly treated with *no*, with negativism." (MFMA, p. 80)

"In every such situation where somebody steps in and takes over, he sows distrust. He hurts the feelings of others for the following reason: Everybody must have some important field in which he is permitted to take care of himself, to live without supervision. And that has been called *the urge to self-determination*. And if that urge to self-determination is thwarted, there results the situation where the person who is thwarted feels a fundamental right is denied him. That fundamental right is to use his own judgment, his own vigilance, his own capabilities. And if this right is denied, then there results what I told you already-distrust, resentment, ill feeling and therefore tenseness." (MFMA, p. 234)

ENDORSEMENT

"What Recovery teaches you, through its philosophy of averageness, is to endorse your successes and to refrain from condemning your failures. An attitude of this kind permits you to accumulate a vast fund of self-endorsement which is made to flow in a running stream from your leading predisposition (philosophy) down to your dispositions for total acts, finally to seep through to each separate position taken in every single part-act." (Selections, p. 47)

"Humans have never been known to endorse themselves as they should." (Selections, p. 132)

"This (self-endorsement) is central to Recovery. So why won't you endorse yourselves? Even God endorsed Himself. Do you remember when He said, 'Let there be Light,' and there was? And after each one of those statements the Bible says, 'And He saw that it was good.' " (MDO, p. 273)

"Any one of you who has conquered one set of symptoms, or more symptoms and some sets of symptoms, has accomplished something that is by no means common. Indeed, it's very rare, except here in Recovery, where it is not rare...Ordinarily if people have nervous symptoms, these nervous symptoms set up vicious cycles, and in time they grow worse and worse, not better. And mark it: you have accomplished your victory over your nervous troubles, not by tricks, not by somebody pulling a trick on you, or you pulling a trick on yourself, but by exercising your will power by means of a method that I have taught you. You owe the conquest over the symptom to your own strength, not to my strength, not to my tricks or stratagems. And why you should not finally get to the point where you acquire pride because of what you have accomplished in your handling of your symptoms-well, I don't know why you don't acquire this pride." (MFMA, p. 33-34)

EXCEPTIONALITY

"If I ask my patients to be realistic instead of sentimental, if I insist that they renounce their romantic sense of exceptionality in favor of sober self-accounting in terms of averageness, I refer to the attitude they are supposed to take with regard to their symptoms. There they must not indulge in sentimental dreams of exceptionality; there they must plant themselves solidly on the ground of realistic averageness." (MHTWT, p. 84-85)

"Even with me who has delivered over 1,500 addresses before Recovery gatherings (twice weekly for fifteen years) there is still some fearful anticipation before each speech and a good deal of unfavorable self-critique afterwards...It is human nature to want superior performance and the perfect achievement...And unless you manage to be saint, angel and wizard combined, you will never succeed in getting rid of your nature. Nature cannot be expelled, but in Recovery we have learned that nature can be controlled." (Selections, p. 124)

"There are very few people who do not think of themselves as being of a superior breed, as ranking above the 'common herd,' that is, as being exceptional. With most of them it is merely a dream, an ambition and aspiration. They hope to be exceptional but know they are 'nothing but average.' In their dreams and fancies they are romanto-intellectuals but in actual practice they behave as realists. Their sense of exceptionality is properly controlled by their knowledge of being average." (MHTWT, p. 248)

"Impulses and feelings are precisely those elements in our experience which balk at being rated as average. They are singularly private and intimate and personal and give you the impression that through them you are set off and distinguished from the others." (MHTWT, p. 250)

"Most if not all people embrace both the philosophy of exceptionality and that of averageness. The average person adjusts and balances the two philosophies in such a manner that the one (averageness) is leading and controlling, the other (exceptionality) is led and controlled. If this is done, then decisions and actions are balanced and adjusted on a practical level while dreams and fancies are given free play on an imaginative level." (MHTWT, p. 248)

"The patients don't drop their desire for perfection, for exceptionality. And why don't they? The reason is simple. People are vain. You and I are vain. Everybody is vain. Do you know what vanity means? Well, I guess you know, but I shall express it in my words. Vanity means I refuse to be like other people. I insist on being better and finer and smarter than other people. I insist on being superior or singular or excellent, and not just average." (MFMA, p. 154)

"Everybody thinks he is the greatest person. He doesn't say so if he's smart. But that's what he feels and thinks and dreams of. And I will give you a slogan which will serve you well: Everybody hopes to be superior and fears to be inferior. That's the picture of human beings." (MFMA, p. 154)

"For anybody to want to be average means to give up the hope of being superior. And people don't like that. They have lived - relatively speaking, the one twenty years and the other thirty and the other sixty - and they have spent their lifetime in dreaming to accomplish greatness. It doesn't have to be the greatness of a presidency of the United States, but to accomplish something exceptional in their group at least, not in humanity. And now they should give up this sixty –year habit. That's a big bill to fill. That's a big order. But here in Recovery you must accept this big order and carry it out." (MFMA, p. 155)

"You want to be superior. This means you depend on others to either recognize you, to give you credit as being not just average, to give you the honor of constantly catering to you, perhaps do you the favor of constantly flattering you. And if you don't get credit and if you don't get honor and if you don't get flattery, then you become tense because you expect it and you don't get it. And therefore vanity and the striving for perfection is harmful, particularly to the nervous patient. Because since vanity is usually not accomplished, since being vain you don't get people to give you the due credit and flattery and honor, therefore you become tense. Vanity always makes you tense. And if you are a nervous patient, and your vanity makes you tense, the tenseness creates symptoms, and you can't get well. At least you can't get well quickly, in due time." (MFMA, p. 155)

"My patients have a special kind of exceptionality. They feel that they are exceptionally wise. They don't know that, but I may tell you they feel that. And so when I say something-when I, for instance, tell a patient, 'Why, don't be so frustrated when I tell you what I told you'-do you understand what that means? I tell the patient that he shows frustration, and such a patient, after I make this statement, is likely to snap back, 'Well, Doctor, I don't feel frustrated.' But how does the patient know that? How does he know what goes on within him? If he knows, why does he come to me to tell him? He consults me precisely about the troubles of his inner life." (MFMA, p. 172-173)

"The patient...has a knowledge of what is in the forefront of his consciousness, but I have the knowledge of what is in the background of his consciousness. I know his inner experiences, and he only knows his outer expression. I wish I could get my patients to realize this. And they don't. I strike against this barrier to fruitfulness, and usefulness, and to improvement, whenever I see the majority of my patients. And why can't I convince them that I know their inner experiences, and they only know their outer expressions on the fringes of consciousness. And I'll tell you why: The reason is that the impulse to show exceptionality-to show superiority, to show great knowledge and the skill of doing things-is inborn." (MFMA, p. 174)

EXPECTATIONS & DISAPPOINTMENTS

"We in Recovery...have asked ourselves, 'Why does the patient get the setback?' and we could not find the answer. We could only find the answer to the question whether the setback can be kept mild or must be degenerating to a severe condition. And you know I have told you, if you expect the setback, if you are sure or convinced that the setback will come, but you can handle it by not being alarmed about it, then the setback will be mild. Otherwise, it will be severe." (MFMA, p. 90)

"To have expectations means to look ahead into the future… Whether your future will be one of fulfillment or of frustration depends on the manner in which you manage your expectations." (Selections, p. 34)

"If your self-appointed expectations meet with frustration and are denied fulfillment, the ensuing disappointment is self-induced, and the responsibility for the defeat is entirely yours. The popular saying, 'As you make your bed so will you lie in it,' refers precisely to this matter of self-appointed expectations leading to self-induced frustrations." (Selections, p. 35)

"Your self-appointed expectations are intuitive productions of your brain…Being pushed back into the background of your consciousness, they are not known to you. You will also understand that the method of getting rid of your harmful and health-wrecking expectations is the proper use of our spotting techniques. What must be spotted is the intuitive meaning of your self-appointments. If your spotting is done correctly, after due Recovery training, you will be able to use your conscious Will for the purpose of saying a resounding "No" to your intuitive strivings and to stop them effectively through control of muscles." (Selections, p. 38)

"If a person expects to live in a world purged of frustrations and obstructions, his extravagant *expectations* will of necessity invite *disappointments*. Then tempers will rise abundantly, and symptoms will not go down rapidly." (Selections, p. 129)

"Whether you check or release your temper depends on how you expect others to behave…men with explosive tempers expect too much consideration from their fellows and view their motives and intentions with too much suspicion." (P v. P, p. 13)

"Patients are fond of thinking that their condition was caused by something external, something in an external environment. And so they have an idea that perhaps if they change environment, it will help them...And some of them go to Florida. Some of them go to California or to Canada, and, well, they feel better when they are there, while they are there. But once they come back to Chicago, their old trouble starts again, and now it is worse because they were disappointed." (MFMA, p. 53)

"If life has no frustration, if life were all happiness and carefree living, then it would be boring. You would be surfeited with a life [of] all smoothness, all proceeding on the same level, no downs, no dips, no frustrations, no disappointments. That is boredom. Expect frustrations all over, all the time. And if you expect them, then you will not be disappointed. Then you will be frustrated, and that will be no disappointment because you expected it." (MFMA, p. 86-87)

EXTREMISM

"Nervous patients tend to be extremists with regard to their symptoms when they are still sick and with regard to the practice of rules after they have improved." (Selections, p. 4)

"In Recovery, the patient is made to realize the fallacy of the romanticist estimate that life is either supreme bliss or dreary desolation. He learns that there is a middle ground of solid averageness in which the tonic quality of realistic action does away with the hectic hunt for picnics which have a sorry way of turning into panics." (Selections, p. 52)

"Will you understand that spotting means primarily to avoid extremes, to avoid extremes above and below...It's a great satisfaction to be satisfied. One doesn't have to be happy. To be in good spirits, why must they be high spirits? And it's not so bad to be dissatisfied. But the patient being dissatisfied immediately says, 'I am the unhappiest person, the unluckiest person, why must everything happen to me?' Haven't you heard that? 'Everything,' the patient speaks in terms of 'everything,' which is nonsense. There are minutes at least when he feels good. But he has the idea things are either always or never. Do you understand these are all extremes?" (MFMA, p. 433)

"If people become enthusiastic about an issue, they tend to make a crusade…and crusaders are dangerous, because they have no sense of proportion." (MFMA, p. 456-457)

"I wish that my patients were a trifle less concerned about their ethics and morals and legality. They are far too concerned about these matters. Instead of having an average concern, they have an extreme concern about them." (MFMA, p. 65-66)

"People have either good habits or bad habits, and what we call *good* is not what we call *moral* or *ethical*. Not at all. People may be ethical and have exaggerated habits of ethical action. That's not good either. They are then dogmatic, aggressive-ethical, but aggressively ethical, fanatically ethical, and that's an extreme. Not good. What we mean by good habits is what I have mentioned as *balanced*. And good habits are balanced habits." (MFMA, p. 229)

FEAR

"If the brain is to conceive fear ideas, they must come to the brain. Seldom will the brain develop these fear ideas out of thin air… The brain must get the impression that there is a situation that connotes danger. But the brain, confronted with an impression of this kind, must accept the impression. It can reject it. Anybody can, with his brain, refuse to believe." (MFMA, p. 348)

"Nervous patients are convinced that what they fear are certain acts or certain occurrences while, in point of fact, the only fear they experience is that of a discomfort which they conceive of as 'unendurable' or 'intolerable' or 'unbearable'. To put it bluntly: nervous fear is the fear of discomfort." (MHTWT, p. 146)

"All you have to do to dispose of a fear is to refuse to believe that there is danger. Then you will ignore it or laugh it out of existence. If you laugh at a thing and ridicule it you cannot possibly fear it. That is the reason why a sense of humor is such a strong antidote against fear." (MHTWT, p. 362)

"The phrase 'I'm scared but I am going anyway' expresses beautifully the very core of Recovery thinking. It is a veritable declaration of independence from sensations, symptoms and panics and a firm determination to let no scares interfere with the realistic business of daily life. Ignoring fears and moving muscles is the essence of courage, will and determination, which means the essence of Recovery thinking." (Selections, p. 106)

"I wish that all my patients performed this little experiment on themselves. When they fear that their dizziness or numbness will lead them to destruction, I wish they would ask themselves the question: If Mr. X had my dizziness or numbness and feared they will kill or cripple him, would I believe that? If you ask this question all the time you might be well all the time." (Selections, p. 127)

"The daily round of the average individual consists, in the main, of such trivial performances as reading, conversing, working on a job, cooking, washing, cleaning, telephoning, shopping…In trivial or routine activities, no calamity arises if perchance a mistake occurs. This is the reason why realists, that is, men and women of average aspirations, go about their daily tasks with due caution and circumspection, it is true, but without any marked fear of making a mistake. Mistakes made in trivial performances are trivial themselves, and their possible consequences are just as trivial and not to be feared." (MHTWT, p. 249)

"Your muscles will not move, of course, if you suggest to them the fear that the movement will lead to disaster. The very thought of disaster ('unendurable' torture) will block motion. Fear even if mild makes muscles tremble and the trepidation thwarts proper execution. If you want your muscles to carry out your commands, you must not scare them into anxiety and hesitation. To strike the muscles with fear and then to ask them to act with precision is absurd. My patients are guilty of this absurdity." (MHTWT, p. 147)

"You will agree that if you fear something you think of that something as a danger. You will also admit that in order to fear a danger you must believe it is real and not imaginary. In other words, you must take the danger seriously and be convinced of its reality." (MHTWT, p. 362)

"You see, the patient has developed a lessened resistance and a high suggestibility. And what does that mean?...If you want to bring a glass of water from one room to the other, and you say, 'Maybe I will spill. Oh, I hope I will not spill,' the muscles don't know this language. But they understand that you are afraid of spilling, that you think you will spill, or may spill, and the muscles become tight. The fear idea makes them tight, and then you will spill. And so it happens with symptoms." (MFMA, p. 385-386)

"There is too much talk about collapses and the danger of heart diseases and the danger of cancer. Cancer is dangerous. I don't deny that. Heart diseases are dangerous. But if you constantly talk and think and hear about the danger of organic diseases, you will not develop an organic disease from this. That will not cause any damage in you. It will, however, cause fear, and the fear will cause a psychological disorder." (MFMA, p. 461)

"Worry may be very useful because if I worry in a real danger, in a realistic danger, well, then I'll take the necessary precautions, and a fear of this kind is useful. Even if a fear turns into a scare, it may still be useful, and frequently is. Suppose I have neglected my work, and then something happens that gives me a shock. I get scared. That scare is useful. It will presumably make me pay more attention to my work. But when the patient is given to fear, there is nothing useful about it. He fears all the time. He develops the habit of fearing. Now, look here: Fear, or distrust, or suspicion, should naturally arise only when there is a danger. And I have yet to see the average person that is always in danger for weeks, and months, and years. Yet my patients, once they conceive a fear, are fearful all the time." (MFMA, p. 7)

"To (a perfectionist)...every puny endeavor, each trivial enterprise is a challenge to prove and to maintain his exceptional stature. His life is a perennial test of his singularity and distinction. For him there are no trivialities, no routine performances. He is forever on trial, before his own inner seat of judgment, for his excellence and exceptional ability. He cannot achieve poise, relaxation, spontaneity. He cannot afford to have the COURAGE TO MAKE MISTAKES. A mistake might wipe out his pretense of being superior, important, exceptional. With no margin left for mistakes he is perpetually haunted by the fear of making them." (MHTWT, p. 250)

"Fear can be remedied only by the certain knowledge that no danger threatens. You cannot gain this knowledge from your own experience which is amateurish and limited to the acquaintance with one single case. What must guide you is my authoritative knowledge which is based on solid study and expert observation. This alone can give you the conviction that no danger whatever attends a night spent in bed even if you feel you 'haven't slept a wink.' " (MHTWT, p. 357)

"My patients are paralyzed by the fear of making mistakes. They are just as good-and in many instances much better-than the average person, but they are afraid to make mistakes." (MFMA, p. 60)

"I walk along in life, and it is clear to me and ought to be clear to everybody, that anybody can at any time fall sick or fall sick again. That will make me feel sad, but it will not make my heart develop palpitations. This means it will not throw me into a great commotion. I will have silent grief, steady perhaps, or interrupted sadness. And grief and sadness do not cause palpitations. If a sad event happens in life, then one should become sad and not frightened." (MFMA, p. 83)

"An average person can have fears and go ahead and act his life regardless of the fear. And that's what you are trained to do in Recovery. In Recovery, we tell you everything that you suffer from – fears, angers, anxieties, pains, pressures – it's all average. And all of these are happenings, accidents, chance events. But now you must exercise something that is not chance but choice, not accident but intention, and that is the will. Have the will to go through your fears and angers and pressures like an average person does or is expected to do. And if you do that, then you will have carried out the main principle of the training which we give here, and, in addition, you will get well." (MFMA, p. 160)

"If you want to get rid of your nervous symptoms, you must establish, or re-establish, relaxation. You can call it peace. You can call it equilibrium. You can call it adjustment, but, essentially, it is relaxation. And if somebody wants to restore relaxation or acquire relaxation, he has to do one thing and that is to banish fear and anger from his system as much as can be done." (MFMA, p. 222)

"Your fear and anger reactions-this means your temperamental reactions-originally do not want to be controlled. They want to express themselves. In fear, you want to run. In anger, you want to strike out. You want to express your anger in an action, this means in an aggressive action. You want to express your fear in an action, that means in a defensive reaction." (MFMA, p. 230)

"I doubt whether I ever heard anybody or saw anybody write a sentence in a book that fear is a belief. I doubt it. At any rate, if it has been done, it happened so seldom that I don't remember having read it. And when it came to me once, well, I can't get my patients rid of fear. How can I do that except over years and years of analysis-you know, that's usually the method-then I began to search for some method that is simpler. And it took me time to find out this trivial truth: that, after all, fear is a belief, the belief that there is danger. Now I knew what to do about fear. If it's a belief, well, then I can train the patient to do what I do every few minutes, certainly every few hours." (MFMA, p. 267)

FEELINGS/EMOTIONS

"Emotions are values, and I do not think of inveighing against them, except in regard to nervous patients and nervous symptoms... if you are seized, as is the case in a panic, with the frustrating emotions of fear, anger and despair, with jealousy and envy, with indignation and disgust, then you must bend all your energies to becoming and remaining cool, chilly, unemotional and objective." (MHTWT, p. 128-129)

"Hate if you have to hate, this means if the feeling of hatred has possessed you; love, of course, if love is there; be jealous if jealousy obsesses you. Be what you are, but don't express feelings of jealousy, feelings of hatred, feelings of anger. The expression can be prevented. And this alone is the object, or is part of the object, of the training which you receive in Recovery." (MFMA, p. 85)

"Recovery, or any other procedure, can never train you how to change the quality of your feelings or how to call upon certain feelings or how to prevent certain feelings from entering your consciousness. So...don't blame yourself for lacking a feeling, or for possessing another feeling that you don't like to possess." (MFMA, p. 85)

"I can't tell you not to feel provoked. I may tell you that I have a great capacity for feeling provoked about every few minutes, but I hope I have an equally great capacity, and perhaps a trifling greater capacity, to hold down the feeling of being provoked." (MFMA, p. 28-29)

"When you claim that your feelings are hurt, what you actually mean is that some cherished belief of yours has been doubted, questioned, ignored, rejected or, worse yet, ridiculed, treated with irony, not taken seriously...hurt feelings...is a misnomer for beliefs not shared." (Selections, p. 20-21)

"Emotions function as a team with intellect as their manager. There are many emotions but there should be one intellect only. This means that intellect must not be *divided* by several conflicting thoughts but must be *determined* by one leading idea. Intellect, as the team manager, determines which member of the emotional team should, at a given moment, be accorded the privilege to release a corresponding act of behavior, and which are to be restrained. If intellect displays managing ability the emotional team will be well balanced." (P v. P, p. 36-37)

"Whatever else may be the meaning of temperamental behavior one thing is plain: underlying it is emotion. There is emotion without temper but there is no temper without emotion." (P v. P, p. 100)

"I want you to know that your feelings are not facts. They merely pretend to reveal facts. Your feelings deceive you. They tell you of danger when there is no hazard, of wakefulness when sleep was adequate, of exhaustion when the body is merely weary and the mind discouraged. In speaking of your symptoms your feelings lie to you. If you trust them you are certain to be betrayed into panics and vicious cycles." (MHTWT, p. 118)

"I said that feelings lie to you, that they deceive and betray you. How can that be? How can feelings be true or false? If you are sad what has that to do with truth, deception or treachery? Feelings are either experienced or they are not. They are present or absent but never true or false. Thoughts alone possess the quality of truth and falseness. And if the patient's feelings tell lies they do so because an incorrect and deceptive thought is attached to them. The deception is accomplished by the thought, not by the feeling." (MHTWT, p. 118)

"If a person is seized with grief or stimulated by joy it would be senseless for the Will to claim that the joy is false or the grief impossible. Feelings are either experienced or not experienced. Their existence, wisdom and probability cannot be denied or affirmed. The same holds for sensations. If the head aches it would be absurd for the Will to object that, 'No, this is no headache. It is unwise, untrue or improbable.' Clearly, if the Will is to intervene in order to control the total experience of insecurity its 'no' cannot be directed to feelings and sensations. Instead, it must address itself to thoughts and impulses." (MHTWT, p. 137)

"I...advise you to reject this contemporary superstition that your thoughts are forever scheming against your welfare and your feelings continually plotting against your health." (MHTWT, p. 140)

"Feelings should be expressed. This does not mean they ought to be acted on or acted out. It merely means they should be communicated to or shared with somebody who can be trusted to understand them…They lend themselves to matter-of-fact discussion and calm appraisal. But temper, involving a claim to being right, cannot be reported objectively, calmly and matter-of-factly. It invariably leads to arguments, debates and rebuttals." (MHTWT, p. 177-178)

"Untold misery is visited on people in general and on my patients in particular, by their belief, by their silly conviction that they are responsible for whatever feelings enter their organism, enter their consciousness." (MFMA, p. 85)

"If somebody says he feels guilty that does not necessarily mean he is guilty. And if somebody feels feverish that does by no means establish the objective fact that he has fever. These examples will prove to you that a subjective feeling does not necessarily point to an objective condition." (MHTWT, p. 338)

"Sensations and feelings rise and fall provided you do not attach the idea of danger at the moment the curve reaches its peak." (MHTWT, p. 356)

"There are subjective facts that the subject feels and objective facts that everybody who has eyes, ears, hands, and certain intelligence can verify. And so the title of that article should read, 'Feelings Are Subjective Facts but Not Objective Facts.' But that title would take up about two lines in the book, and we don't want that. Therefore, we merely let it read, 'Feelings Are Not Facts.' But you should supplement in your mind the adjective *objective* and say, 'Feelings Are Not Objective Facts.' " (MFMA, p. 78)

"I walk along in life, and it is clear to me and ought to be clear to everybody, that anybody can at any time fall sick or fall sick again. That will make me feel sad, but it will not make my heart develop palpitations. This means it will not throw me into a great commotion. I will have silent grief, steady perhaps, or interrupted sadness. And grief and sadness do not cause palpitations. If a sad event happens in life, then one should become sad and not frightened." (MFMA, p. 83)

"If somebody should hate any other person, in-law or not, because that person has been very unfriendly to the one who now hates him, I would not consider this a verdict on the character or the personality of that hating person. I will not approve of it, but I will say this is an average reaction." (MFMA, p. 84)

"All your feelings, including your feelings about your symptoms, which are thoroughly individualistic, should be held down. They should be controlled. You should not pamper them, and coddle them, and not constantly think of them as being so dangerous and so overpowering. And that's what we call in Recovery *controlling your self-importance*." (MFMA, p. 256)

FRUSTRATION

"If life has no frustration, if life were all happiness and carefree living, then it would be boring. You would be surfeited with a life [of] all smoothness, all proceeding on the same level, no downs, no dips, no frustrations, no disappointments. That is boredom. Expect frustrations all over, all the time. And if you expect them, then you will not be disappointed. Then you will be frustrated, and that will be no disappointment because you expected it." (MFMA, p. 86-87)

"Frustrations mean life. A dead body cannot be frustrated. They mean life, and I doubt whether I ever passed through ten minutes in my adult life in which I did not feel frustrated. So they must mean life, these frustrations. If there is nothing outside me to frustrate me, be sure there is plenty inside me with which I am disgusted and dissatisfied and over which I am disappointed. And where is the person that is so happily placed that he can spend many ten minute periods without criticizing him[self], without being dissatisfied with him[self], and disappointed over what he remembers or looks forward to. Believe me, that's no exaggeration. Life is a continuous frustration. Fortunately, most of the frustration is mild if one is well, if one is reasonably adjusted not only in health but in habit." (MFMA, p. 212)

"I don't know anything else in life that can be frustrated except an impulse. You may say that there are beliefs, and strivings, and ambitions that can be frustrated. But they are all based on an impulse. And you may take it on trust that if something is frustrated, it is always an impulse no matter by what name you call it." (MFMA, p. 276)

"Frustration is certainly average. It's not only average, it is common, continuous, more or less, only interrupted by some fleeting moment, sometimes by a fleeting hour, sometimes by an afternoon in which there is great excitement...and all a human being can do is to hold the continuous series of frustrations down to a low level. In other words, he cannot avoid the millions of frustrations that are awaiting for him in the course of a certain time." (MFMA, p. 47)

"I want to tell you something about the method with which frustrations can be held down to a low intensity, without raising their number and their duration. It is a simple prescription that I will offer to you. The prescription reads, 'If you deal with everyday life, with routine work or routine existence, if you deal with the trivialities of the daily round, don't believe that they are emergencies.'" (MFMA, p. 47)

"My patients think of their troubles-of their frustrations, especially the frustrations that come from symptoms, and they are indeed sharp and severe-they think of them as emergencies. And if you think of an event as an emergency, then what happens is clear. You work yourself up over it, you become panicky, you become hopeless, and the frustration reaches proportions that are overwhelming, and life is no longer worth living." (MFMA, p. 48)

GOALS

"The one and only goal of the patient must be to regain his mental health. In order to achieve it, the goals and whims and wishes of "human nature" must be held down with ruthless determination." (MHTWT, p. 218-219)

"My purpose in life is to make myself and those people that are close to me-let me say the members of my family, my friends, my neighbors, and so forth, my co-workers-to make them feel good and to make myself feel good." (MFMA, p. 109)

"When you are ill your main and all-absorbing purpose must be the will to get well. All other purposes, no matter how inspiring and exalted, must be subordinated to the one leading and supreme purpose of getting well and keeping well. Unless you regain and maintain your mental health all other purposes will be frustrated." (MHTWT, p. 407)

"Having lost control over the functions of the nervous system the patient consults the physician asking him to supply the leadership that he himself can no longer provide. Physician and patient are now forming a partnership in which a unified purpose is set and defined by the physician and accepted by the patient. In this partnership the physician represents the group purpose of mental health and self-discipline. The patient accepts it and pledges himself to employ all the necessary means to attain the end." (MHTWT, p. 281-282)

"The nervous patient must not permit himself the luxury of employing a confusing terminology. To him it must be clear that the PURPOSE AIMS AT ITS GOAL. He must then be shown with unquestioned clarity which is the purpose that moves him, which the goal he has set for himself and what is the degree of determination with which he must aim at the goal." (MHTWT, p. 287)

"All significant action must be so contrived that it aims at the chosen goal. The aiming must be effective, i.e., straight, direct, sustained, determined, energetic. It must not be wavering, ambiguous, capricious, hesitating, irresolute." (MHTWT, p. 288)

"Once the physician has made the diagnosis of a nervous ailment a goal is set for the patient to aim at…The goal is that of self-discipline. What must be disciplined is the patient's behavior, particularly his behavior toward his inner experiences." (MHTWT, p. 295)

"A person endowed with character aims at his long range group goals (values) either with rigid, unyielding *principles* or with elastic but firm *policies*. Principles admit of no exception, policies do. It is unprincipled behavior to steal or cheat even once. But it may be a good policy to relax discipline frequently in dealing with children or employees. Principles call for relentlessness, severity, perhaps even for fanaticism; policies call for a flexible strategy, for maneuver and careful adjustment to the requirements of the just prevailing situation. But no matter how fundamentally different they are with regard to rigidity and flexibility both principle and policy defeat their purpose unless they are acted on with steadfastness, determination, patience and sustained effort." (MHTWT, p. 303)

"The fact is that health does not seem to be considered a value in its own right. The other fact, however, is that without health there can be no proper aiming at long range goals and their corresponding values. The functions of loyal service, religious devotion, patriotic duty, parenthood, friendship, sociability, civic-mindedness cannot be accomplished if the individual is crippled, bed ridden or otherwise seriously handicapped. That functions of this order cannot be properly discharged if they are continuously frustrated by frightening sensations, panics, and anxieties needs no comment. Mental health particularly is not only a value. It is a necessary prerequisite for the unhampered functioning of all the values represented in the table of valuations." (MHTWT, p. 303-304)

"Mistakes of judgment can be made either by way of setting yourself a mistaken goal or by picking mistaken means for the goal that may be good." (MFMA, p. 221)

"The group wants you to do what you need, not what you want… the group has one goal, and the individual has another goal. The group is not in the way of the individual, but it's not interested in it. If you want to take a swim, the group is not against it, but the group is definitely against it if you want to take a swim while some task waits to be performed. The group wants you to discharge your obligations. But the individual, when he is in trouble, has inclinations, the inclination to get relief." (MFMA, p. 274)

"If I have now the impulse, or the wish, or desire to ask for help, then I naturally want to get this help immediately, right now, if I suffer severely. And that's what we call the short-range goal. The goal that is now in the patient's mind is meant to bring something on this minute. It's a momentary, short-range goal…My goal that I set before the patient is not meant to get into action or to be reached this moment. It is meant to be reached in weeks or months. So the goal that I have set for the patient is a long-range goal. But the patient who suffers now is not particularly interested in what is going to happen in five, six, or ten months. He wants relief now and not a minute later. And you will now understand that that's what the patient wants. That's his want but the goal that I set for him is his need." (MFMA, p. 286)

GROUP-MINDEDNESS

"The common frustrations of daily life can be borne and remedied by a sense of humor. It takes a sense of humor to think of one's self and one's frustrations as average. The philosophy of Recovery is opposed to the sense of self-importance and favors the sense of group-importance. The knowledge that 'I am not so important' creates a sense of humor." (Selections, p. 110)

"'Rights' is a term borrowed from the business field of competition and domination and ought to have no place in the home which is the domain of service and cooperation." (P v. P, p. 95)

"In a group (marriage, friendship, business partnership) there are two principal goal ideas: cooperation or competition, mutuality or rivalry. The feeling of fellowship, linked to the goal ideas of cooperation and mutuality, gives rise to the *will to peace*. The feeling of self-importance, linked to the goal ideas of competition or rivalry, yields the *will to power*. The will to peace makes for understanding, the will to power for misunderstanding." (P v. P, p. 195)

"In group life, an insincere gesture of generosity and fellowship is far more valuable than an outspoken expression of enmity and a brutal assertion of one's sovereignty." (MHTWT, p. 59)

"A patient and his physician are, of course, an intimate group, at any rate with regard to health. And health is the major concern of you. So I and you form an intimate group. And in this group, that has as its characteristics closeness and intimacy, in this group, if it is to be intimate, there must take place one factor without which there can't be intimacy. And that is mutual understanding. Without mutual understanding, there is no intimacy. And mutual understanding means that somebody whom I want to understand and to whom I want to understand me, we two-the somebody and I-must have approximately the same views. They must have, in other words, the same outlook, the same approach, not in every respect but in important respects." (MFMA, p. 129-130)

"No patient, to my knowledge, has ever turned against the group with a knife or with a gun. I haven't seen it. Maybe there are some. But the patient has turned frequently and almost regularly, while he has been suffering, against the group with his mouth or his tongue. And you may say that a gun is more dangerous than a tongue, but not necessarily so. A tongue may be very offensive and therefore dangerous to the individual himself...what he says may cause offense and may antagonize the people he talks to and then again rebound to his disadvantage. The impulse that he thought will serve him is a boomerang and harms because the impulse, if expressed, offends those around the patient." (MFMA, p. 167-168)

"Whenever you reach the point where most of your actions are controlled and only part of your actions are easily expressed, then you have balance...and that is that kind of balance in which the group reactions predominate over the individualistic reactions, and that's the only kind of balance we want in life: the balance in which control predominates over reckless expression." (MFMA, p. 231)

"In life it is so arranged, or it should be so arranged, that the group feelings overbalance the individualistic feelings without eliminating them. The individualistic feelings are our nature, and they should not be eliminated because they can't be eliminated. They are our nature, and you can't eliminate nature. But they should be kept under control. This means the group feelings and group entities should have a preponderance over the individualistic entities. The group feelings, in other words, should just overbalance the individual feelings, but the individualistic feelings must remain. You can't eradicate them. You can't throw them out of your body. They remain with you from birth to the grave. There is nothing to be done about nature except to control it. And that's what you learn here." (MFMA, p. 255-256)

"Let me tell you, the setbacks to which a nervous patient is liable are mainly caused by the renewed tenseness that comes from a renewed temper, which stems from the renewed importance that you give yourself-again, self-importance. And if you have learned the distinction between self-importance and group importance in relation to tenseness and symptoms, well, then you have indeed learned a great deal." (MFMA, p. 256)

"The group wants you to do what you need, not what you want… the group has one goal, and the individual has another goal. The group is not in the way of the individual, but it's not interested in it. If you want to take a swim, the group is not against it, but the group is definitely against it if you want to take a swim while some task waits to be performed. The group wants you to discharge your obligations. But the individual, when he is in trouble, has inclinations, the inclination to get relief." (MFMA, p. 274)

"Training means to make the muscles which carry out your impulses, to make the muscles carry out those impulses only that are in accord with a leading principle. If your leading principle is to adjust to a group, and you mean it, then you will not permit your muscles to carry out a crime. That's out of the question. The impulse will be there, but [you] will not permit it to see the light of the day." (MFMA, p. 281)

HABITS

"Gossip is a mechanism capable of relieving the tenseness caused by conflicts. It gives relief by convincing you that the 'other fellow' is wrong, so atrociously wrong that your failing in this respect must appear very small, indeed. Bullying, sarcasm, ridicule are other such mechanisms. They all tend to demonstrate the wrongness, weakness, helplessness, and inadequacy of others. After bullying, ridiculing, or reprimanding others you have the doubtful distinction of having scored a victory. It is this sense of being victorious that gives you the pleasure of which I spoke when I stated that poor manners are cultivated and permitted to become set habits 'because a premium of secret pleasure is placed on them'." (P v. P, p. 82-83)

"If anybody, any one of you, has the infantile idea that you just can manage to hear that there is no danger, and then you think you understand it, and therefore it will be settled in your brain, well, that is wish thinking. I hear plenty of things, and I understand them, and then I go ahead and still practice the habits that I have acquired, although I know now that they are not of the best. That happens to everybody because everybody has harmful habits." (MFMA, p. 9)

"I am not at all concerned with your being natural and human. My sole objective is to rid you of your symptoms. You seem to think it is your natural and human privilege to exercise your temper. It is just as natural and human to eat steak. But if a man is suffering from a gastric upset he'd better relinquish his 'natural and human right' to steak dinners. Are you willing to give up your temper for the sake of your health?" (MHTWT, p. 387)

"Everybody develops habits. When I was a boy, I was awful. I was a nail biter. I bit my nails. That went on for years and years. What did I get out of it? Nothing. Nothing but annoyance, embarrassment, a sense of shame! Tremendous incentive to stop it! It looked ugly. Could I make up my mind to stop it and it stopped? It took years and years. It was a habit." (MDO, p. 144)

"I hope that you will go home now-after having some refreshments, of course-and will give some thought to what you have heard me say. And if you do, don't expect that from now on you will change, even if you give careful thought to what I have told you and what is only a repetition of what I used to tell you and have told you so many times…Once you make up your mind you want to change, in order to change, you must undergo training, and that takes time. And please don't become disappointed if you make up your mind today to use your sense of humor, and you find out that tomorrow that you have not used it. Well, that's perfectly average and human." (MFMA, p. 100)

"For anybody to want to be average means to give up the hope of being superior. And people don't like that. They have lived - relatively speaking, the one twenty years and the other thirty and the other sixty - and they have spent their lifetime in dreaming to accomplish greatness. It doesn't have to be the greatness of a presidency of the United States, but to accomplish something exceptional in their group at least, not in humanity. And now they should give up this sixty-year habit. That's a big bill to fill. That's a big order. But here in Recovery you must accept this big order and carry it out." (MFMA, p. 155)

"Poor habits can be acquired in a fraction of a second, good habits only in long, protracted training." (MFMA, p. 216)

"I deal with patients, and therefore I am, of course, partial to the notion of training. How can a patient get well unless he establishes the habit of control of his impulses, control of his temper, control of his keen desire to make his own diagnosis, control of his desire to constantly check his body and find out the spots that he thinks are decaying or rotting? If I don't establish new habits in him, then how can he get well? How can he acquire, then, the habits that he needs?" (MFMA, p. 217-218)

"If people are trained in the acquisition of habits, then it's understood they must go on training and training with perseverance, with determination, and training without letup. *Trying* means immediately something that the patient doesn't know he has expressed. It means immediately, 'I don't know whether I can do it.' This means a determination not to put up too much effort" (MFMA, p. 218)

"People have either good habits or bad habits, and what we call *good* is not what we call *moral* or *ethical*. Not at all. People may be ethical and have exaggerated habits of ethical action. That's not good either. They are then dogmatic, aggressive--ethical, but aggressively ethical, fanatically ethical, and that's an extreme. Not good. What we mean by good habits is what I have mentioned as *balanced*. And good habits are balanced habits." (MFMA, p. 229)

"If you want to gain good control and good ability of spotting, then you must turn spotting into a habit, and you can't acquire a habit in two days, not in two weeks. If you acquire it in two years, then you are very lucky." (MFMA, p. 232)

"A symptom is a new habit that the patient has developed through tenseness." (MFMA, p. 235)

"It's a simple method. You just tell somebody to drop his belief, and he could do it. It's simple, but he doesn't drop it. He keeps his belief. And if I want the patient to drop beliefs, well, he makes an effort, but they don't work. They certainly don't work immediately. And there was one thing that I forgot about…when I formulated this theory: I forgot the fact that humans develop habits, and habits are stubborn." (MFMA, p. 268)

HELPLESSNESS/HOPELESSNESS

"With the spread of specialism, self-help and self-management have ceased to play a significant part in the present-day domestic, marital and social scene. The habit of rushing to the expert for advice has resulted in a vicious cycle of helplessness: the more the expert's aid is solicited the more helpless is the applicant bound to feel; the greater the helplessness the more urgent the need for further consultations; the more frequent the consultations the more poignant the sense of helplessness. In the end, an individual emerges who has a stunted Will, a meager 'know-how', and a famished sense of resourcefulness, in short, Modern Man, the pathetic creature of an extraneous Will, without plans or directions of his own and in abject dependence on forces outside his inner self." (MHTWT, p. 143-144)

"I have not seen a patient who was not helpless, totally or partially. Patients are helpless to stop their pressures, they are helpless when they find themselves seized with air-hunger or night terror. And if any patient claims to be helpless I shall not challenge the correctness of his statement. But when a patient declares himself hopeless I shall warn him that he has presumed to make a prognosis and has trespassed into my territory. The physician alone is capable of deciding whether a condition is hopeless or hopeful." (MHTWT, p. 96)

"Once you call your condition a condition that can't be helped-this means that it is either untreatable or incurable-well, then you naturally develop a scare, alarm; you become hopeless, and you work up tenseness...And those of you that are regular customers here know that to cut out tenseness means don't make a disastrous diagnosis. Don't diagnose insecurity, incurability, untreatability. Diagnose as I have done. Accept as I have done." (MFMA, p. 370)

"What the patient wants his listener to be convinced of is that he is a helpless victim of his symptoms; that he tries everything within his power to be calm but does not succeed; that he is trapped by his handicap and cannot escape its grip. His tantrums, his bursts of dizziness, his weakness and fatigue, his tremors and palpitations, he thinks, are all of one cast: they are beyond endurance and beyond control. These complaints lack conviction because they are grossly contradicted by the facts of daily observation." (MHTWT, p. 204-205)

"Even if you have been a nervous patient for thirty and thirty-five and forty years-and I have seen them-even then, once you learn how to relax and to throw off fears, nature is certain to repair the complication." (MFMA, p. 16)

"Here in Recovery we have finally made it clear to the patients-and sometimes we have made it clear to the world-that even if a patient has reached that final stage that is largely featured in the textbooks, we are not afraid of it. And therefore we go ahead, take care of these patients, restore them to health in a great number of instances. And, as a further consequence, we have therefore adopted the slogan, 'There are no hopeless cases among nervous patients, regardless of the final duration of the condition.'" (MFMA, p. 211)

HUMOR

"A sense of humor...is the sovereign means for curing nervous conditions." (MFMA, p. 97)

"All you have to do to dispose of a fear is to refuse to believe that there is danger. Then you will ignore it or laugh it out of existence. If you laugh at a thing and ridicule it you cannot possibly fear it. That is the reason why a sense of humor is such a strong antidote against fear." (MHTWT, p. 362)

"The common frustrations of daily life can be borne and remedied by a sense of humor. It takes a sense of humor to think of one's self and one's frustrations as average. The philosophy of Recovery is opposed to the sense of self-importance and favors the sense of group-importance. The knowledge that 'I am not so important' creates a sense of humor." (Selections, p. 110)

"To be able to laugh at a thing means to refuse to take it seriously. The trouble with the ill-bred individual is that he takes his stirrings, his conflicts, and fears ridiculously seriously. The well-bred person has a sense of humor; the ill-mannered person lacks it." (P v. P, p. 84)

"I hope that these lectures will make it possible for you to laugh at your paltry conflicts, to smile at your fear of not being right, and to joke at your urge to prove others wrong. If you manage to do that your conflicts, fears and apprehensions will be relieved, and the recovered patient will return to a home pervaded by the spirit of patience and forbearance and a-sense of humor." (P v. P, p. 84)

"You will agree that if you fear something you think of that something as a danger. You will also admit that in order to fear a danger you must believe it is real and not imaginary. In other words, you must take the danger seriously and be convinced of its reality. All you have to do to dispose of a fear is to refuse to believe that there is danger. Then you will ignore it or laugh it out of existence. If you laugh at a thing and ridicule it you cannot possibly fear it. That is the reason why a sense of humor is such a strong antidote against fear." (MHTWT, p. 362)

"Sometimes I lie down and daydream and then I have all kinds of fantasies how important I will be some day. Well, it will be about time if it should materialize. I'm not just getting younger, you know. And then all of a sudden after a minute or two I remind myself, 'Well, that's all nonsense, why should I dream about greatness and glamour and fame and fortune and so forth?' and then I stop because it appears ridiculous to me. I have applied a sense of humor." (MDO, p. 143-144)

"The sense of shame, of fear, of hatred, of contempt applied to trivialities of life have this in common: that they are utterly out of the range of humor. A person hating trivialities, fearing trivialities, being ashamed of daily trivialities, has, of course, no sense of humor. And my patients, as long as they are suffering from their panics, from their frightful sensations and impulses, and so forth, have, of course, no sense of humor. They take their inner experiences too seriously." (MFMA, p. 96-97)

"Do you understand now that having a good sense of humor and feeling average are the same thing? And looking on his troubles with a great sense of importance is the same thing as having no sense of humor. So, this matter of importance is opposed to the matter of averageness, and the sense of humor is opposed, naturally, to the sense of importance." (MFMA, p. 99)

IMPULSES

"When I have an impulse, be certain I did not summon it. I did not call it into being. I didn't make any effort to get this impulse started, especially if it is an impulse that I hate, that I don't want. Then be certain I am not responsible for it. This means I didn't create it. I didn't do anything to bring it to the fore. So why should I blame myself? Why should I feel disgraced?...And...that's what all of you do." (MFMA, p. 450)

"Impulses and feelings are precisely those elements in our experience which balk at being rated as average. They are singularly private and intimate and personal and give you the impression that through them you are set off and distinguished from the others." (MHTWT, p. 250)

"It [the impulse] always comes by Fate. I get such impulses, much more dreadful impulses. But my nerves have been steeled and trained to develop resistance, and when dreadful and mischievous and lascivious and blasphemous impulses reach my brain, I look away and wait and they will depart. And they depart in no time because my resistance has been strengthened and Fate is not strong enough to break my resistance once it is strengthened through training." (MDO, p. 144)

"I don't know anything else in life that can be frustrated except an impulse. You may say that there are beliefs, and strivings, and ambitions that can be frustrated. But they are all based on an impulse. And you may take it on trust that if something is frustrated, it is always an impulse no matter by what name you call it." (MFMA, p. 276)

"Training means to make the muscles which carry out your impulses, to make the muscles carry out those impulses only that are in accord with a leading principle. If your leading principle is to adjust to a group, and you mean it, then you will not permit your muscles to carry out a crime. That's out of the question. The impulse will be there, but [you] will not permit it to see the light of the day." (MFMA, p. 281)

INNER & OUTER ENVIRONMENT

"Events in outer environment, and even in inner environment, are routine in the overwhelming majority of instances." (MFMA, p. 108)

"What is of importance is not the event but the attitude that you take to the event…The attitude is yours…and…can be controlled, can be changed, can be improved…The event usually cannot." (MFMA, p. 108)

"We live in the age of technique and boast that we have conquered time and space and matter and nature…But of what good are conquests if they play solely in the field of external environment, leaving internal environment prostrate and helpless to be ravaged by the onslaughts of unbridled tempers?…control of our internal environment is infinitely more important than all the possible triumphs we may be able to score over external environment." (MHTWT, p. 110)

"Temper is the bridge over which environmental irritations can reach across the muscles to the inner organs and to the depth of the personality. Along this road it penetrates to the domain which we call internal environment." (MHTWT, p. 107)

"Of what good is your automobile if all it has brought you is the possibility of experiencing your palpitation at a speed of fifty miles an hour? Are you interested in external speed or in inner peace? You hear it stated these days on every street corner and in every newspaper column that moral progress has not kept pace with technological advance. Well, it is truer to say that the emphasis on technological progress made us forget the importance of progressing in the domain of morale. Recovery has reversed the proportion, and the reversed position was given beautiful expression by the members of the panel. To us at any rate, control of our internal environment is infinitely more important than all the possible triumphs we may be able to score over external environment." (MHTWT, p. 110)

"Environment is not constantly threatening. Environment changes. And if you feel constantly insecure, that cannot refer to any reality or any real danger in [the] environment. That can only be a sense of [in}security that has developed into a senseless habit apart from any danger in environment." (MFMA, p. 8)

"Once you think of yourself as being a victim, you will not try to seek help from your inner environment, from yourself." (MFMA, p. 49-50)

"Patients are fond of thinking that their condition was caused by something external, something in an external environment. And so they have an idea that perhaps if they change environment, it will help them...And some of them go to Florida. Some of them go to California or to Canada, and, well, they feel better when they are there, while they are there. But once they come back to Chicago, their old trouble starts again, and now it is worse because they were disappointed." (MFMA, p. 53)

"In Recovery you are told that if you want to get well, you have to influence your internal environment-your internal environment that consists mainly of impulses, sensations, obsessions, that must be controlled as you learn here. And, second, of your beliefs, that must be changed according to the standards that you are taught here." (MFMA, p. 56)

INNER RESPONSES & OUTER REACTIONS

"In point of *inner responses* men are alike. They differ only in their readiness to convert their inner responses into *open reactions*. The realist is inclined to control his feeling and thought responses; the romantic and intellectual tend to express them." (MHTWT, p. 76)

"Recovery denies emphatically that any inner experience of the nervous patients is irresistible. It knows of situations only that *were not resisted.* This refers to common everyday experiences, the common tantrum, the common crying spell, the common anger and common fear. All of them can be resisted, none are irresistible." (MHTWT, p. 181)

"Your fear and anger reactions-this means your temperamental reactions-originally do not want to be controlled. They want to express themselves. In fear, you want to run. In anger, you want to strike out. You want to express your anger in an action, this means in an aggressive action. You want to express your fear in an action, that means in a defensive reaction." (MFMA, p. 230)

"It is good to know what temper means. And...let me tell you it means many things, but one thing I wish to discuss today, particularly. Temper is an act-an act. You speak in temper; you distort your features, and all of these are acts. You perhaps move your arms. You flash your eyes. You perhaps blanche or get red in the face. All of these are acts. And an act has this characteristic, that it begins with an intention." (MFMA, p. 244)

INSECURITY/SECURITY

"It is the tragedy of the nervous patient that after years of suffering he develops an unbalanced imagination, the first guesses of which tend distressingly and consistently to interpret inner and outer experiences in terms of insecurity. The greater tragedy is that the first guesses are accepted sight unseen without an attempt at verification. Unable to resist its suggestions the patient becomes the victim of the imagination." (MHTWT, p. 38)

"Barring certain organic diseases, no human experience is possible, even thinkable, in which thoughts express security and impulses are restless and erratic." (MHTWT, p. 135)

"What stimulates muscles is courage and self-confidence, that means, the sense of security. What frustrates them is fear and self-distrust, that is, the sense of insecurity." (MHTWT, p. 370)

"Ordinarily, no act of yours will be released unless the brain first takes the view that no danger is involved. After the brain has, in the flash of a momentary decision, reached the conclusion that the situation is one of security it stimulates the muscles to release the appropriate act. The conclusion that the planned act is safe is formed without your conscious knowledge. We say it is arrived at intuitively and not discursively." (MHTWT, p. 371)

"In order to check the idea of insecurity the first step to be taken by the self-conscious person will have to be to practice in an environment in which the chances of being misunderstood or underrated are at their lowest. This is one of the reasons, as you know, why I insist that my patients associate with their fellow-sufferers in Recovery. There they have an opportunity to attack their fears and suspicions where they are weakest. I hope you realize now that if you wish to get rid of your troubles you will have to adopt this well tried method which means that you will have to attack those of your symptoms first which form the weakest links in the chain of your ill-balanced sensations, feelings and impulses." (MHTWT, p. 382)

"Environment is not constantly threatening. Environment changes. And if you feel constantly insecure, that cannot refer to any reality or any real danger in [the] environment. That can only be a sense of [in}security that has developed into a senseless habit apart from any danger in environment." (MFMA, p. 8)

INTENTIONS

"It is good to know what temper means. And...let me tell you it means many things, but one thing I wish to discuss today, particularly. Temper is an act-an act. You speak in temper; you distort your features, and all of these are acts. You perhaps move your arms. You flash your eyes. You perhaps blanche or get red in the face. All of these are acts. And an act has this characteristic, that it begins with an intention." (MFMA, p. 244)

"Before you act, you intend to do something. Whether it's done consciously, whether the intention is conscious or intuitive-this means *subconscious*, you can call it-does not matter. There is always a conscious or an intuitive or an instinctive intention." (MFMA, p. 244)

LITERALNESS

"Nervous patients tend to be extremists with regard to their symptoms when they are still sick and with regard to the practice of rules after they have improved." (Selections, p. 4)

MOTIONLESS SITTING

"I have again yet to see the person who, if he applies this mechanism of motionless sitting as I want it applied, I have yet to see that patient who doesn't get sustained relief from it for a far longer period than can be measured in seconds…A steadying of the body, by means of motionless sitting, gives instant relief which at first is brief, but then lengthens and lengthens and produces a real sustained relief." (MFMA, p. 288-289)

MUSCLE CONTROL

"The best means of reducing an idea of danger to its absurdity is to act against it." (MHTWT, p. 366-367)

"Muscles always carry out orders that are meant-orders which are resolutely passed on to them." (MHTWT, p. 333)

"Hate if you have to hate, this means if the feeling of hatred has possessed you; love, of course, if love is there; be jealous if jealousy obsesses you. Be what you are, but don't express feelings of jealousy, feelings of hatred, feelings of anger. The expression can be prevented. And this alone is the object, or is part of the object, of the training which you receive in Recovery." (MFMA, p. 85)

"My patients are asked to use their muscles primarily for the control of sensations, and more so yet, perhaps, for the control of obsessions and compulsions." (MFMA, p. 313)

"Harriette learned in Recovery that if the brain defaulted on its managerial duties, the muscles can be made to 'take over' and to 'pinch-hit' for the cringing cerebral manager…the resoluteness of the muscles would conquer the defeatism of the brain." (MFMA, p. 65-66)

"I can't tell you not to feel provoked. I may tell you that I have a great capacity for feeling provoked about every few minutes, but I hope I have an equally great capacity, and perhaps a trifling greater capacity, to hold down the feeling of being provoked." (MFMA, p. 28-29)

"Suffering can either be reported objectively or complained about subjectively...Stop the muscular habit of complaining, and you will put an end to the mental habit of defeatism." (Selections, p. 45)

"The phrase 'I'm scared but I am going anyway' expresses beautifully the very core of Recovery thinking. It is a veritable declaration of independence from sensations, symptoms and panics and a firm determination to let no scares interfere with the realistic business of daily life. Ignoring fears and moving muscles is the essence of courage, will and determination, which means the essence of Recovery thinking." (Selections, p. 106)

"There are so many things I do not understand that it would be physically impossible to catalogue them. I do not understand why, on some morning I arise and find myself devoid of my customary energy, or why on some occasions I am sprightly and mentally alert and on other occasions my spirit seems to have gone from me and my disposition reaches a low ebb of dullness and indolence that is truly appalling. And I do not understand at all why if I have some unfathomable difficulty it lasts five minutes the one day and two or three hours the other. All of this is beyond my comprehension. Fortunately, it is immaterial whether a nervous condition is or is not understood. What counts is the knowledge that every nervous symptom, no matter how mysterious and incomprehensible, can be controlled through spotting thoughts and commanding muscles. You see, no matter what subject you patients will bring up, my answer is invariably and monotonously: Spot your thoughts and command your muscles!" (Selections, p. 115-116)

"You may have difficulty controlling fears and worries. But muscles can be controlled 'at will.' Everybody has it within his power to command his muscles to effect an act or to refrain from effecting it." (MHTWT, p. 350)

"Everybody speaks of the brain as governing behavior. That's all nonsense. The brain plays quite some part in behavior, but not the principal part; the principal part is played by the muscles. The brain influences the muscles, there is no doubt. But the muscles can influence the brain much more...particularly with patients." (MFMA, p. 332)

"If you are one of those patients that in the morning feel limp, devitalized, tired, exhausted-and you know I have quite a few of these patients-and then you make up your mind, regardless of how tired you are, how limp you feel, how lifeless you are, regardless of all of this, you will jump out of bed and do things, then you have scored a victory...if a patient does that, he has definitely gained a victory over a formidable enemy, that is, his incapacity. Why is he not proud of himself?" (MFMA, p. 31-32)

"With regard to that variety of knowledge and experience that tells you what to do and what not to do there can be hardly any doubt that the *muscles are pre-eminently the teachers and educators of the brain*...Muscles teach the brain, and the brain, enriched by knowledge, guides the muscles." (MHTWT, p. 66-67)

"Beliefs are frequently stubborn and obstinate...Muscles are just as likely to develop obstinacy. They tend to acquire set patterns of behavior preferring certain well grooved acts and avoiding others. Just think of the habits of procrastination, of twitches and spasms, of restlessness and sluggishness, and you will realize that muscles are not always pliant tools in the hands of the Will. In order to pry loose the resisting beliefs and rebellious muscles attempt after attempt must be made to dislodge them from their comfortable berth and to force them to give up resistance. The resistance may be so strong that the attempts to break it must be repeated in innumerable trials before success is achieved. This requires the Will to use a great deal of power in continued strenuous practice." (MHTWT, p. 141-142)

"Your muscles will not move, of course, if you suggest to them the fear that the movement will lead to disaster. The very thought of disaster ('unendurable' torture) will block motion. Fear even if mild makes muscles tremble and the trepidation thwarts proper execution. If you want your muscles to carry out your commands you must not scare them into anxiety and hesitation. To strike the muscles with fear and then to ask them to act with precision is absurd. My patients are guilty of this absurdity." (MHTWT, p. 147)

"Whatever else a disturbing nervous symptom may mean, its main effect is that it interferes with the adjustment of the patient. And adjustment is effected through action, and action is carried on through muscles, including the muscles of speech…Nothing is more convincing that muscular performance." (MHTWT, p. 325)

"What stimulates muscles is courage and self-confidence, that means, the sense of security. What frustrates them is fear and self-distrust, that is, the sense of insecurity." (MHTWT, p. 370)

"Ordinarily, no act of yours will be released unless the brain first takes the view that no danger is involved. After the brain has, in the flash of a momentary decision, reached the conclusion that the situation is one of security it stimulates the muscles to release the appropriate act. The conclusion that the planned act is safe is formed without your conscious knowledge. We say it is arrived at intuitively and not discursively." (MHTWT, p. 371)

Dr. Low to a patient: "Once you commanded your speech muscles to move the very action of the muscles had a vitalizing effect on the brain. The movement of the muscles convinced the brain that speaking is possible. And when the brain witnessed the living, vital performance of the muscles it acquired a new vitality itself and lost its lifelessness. The more forceful was the action of the muscles the more vitalized became the brain; the more vital the brain the more forceful the muscles. By commanding your muscles to move you had thus transformed the *vicious cycle of helplessness* into the *vitalizing cycle of self-confidence*." (MHTWT, p. 374)

"Spontaneity is interfered with or destroyed by self-consciousness…

self-consciousness is produced by the fact that two contradictory intentions endeavor to make the muscles express two different ideas at the same time. The muscles are thrown into disorder expressing portions of the one idea and fragments of the other with the result that the speech loses clarity and gives the impression of confusion." (MHTWT, p. 413-414)

"If muscles get two contradictory orders at the same time, all they can do is to create tenseness or to begin to tremble or to stiffen up or all three together. And then there is no action. And you will understand that the patient can in this manner confuse the muscles, irritate them, throwing them into tenseness and spasms and in tremors. This means making them react like you react in temper: tenseness, stiffness. And that's what the muscles do, and then there is no leadership. The person doesn't exercise guidance, doesn't give guidance. And if this happens, the person notices that the muscles don't do as he wants them to do, so he now becomes more irritated, more suspicious that there may be something wrong with him, and therefore more temperamental. And a vicious cycle develops." (MFMA, p. 117)

"No patient, to my knowledge, has ever turned against the group with a knife or with a gun. I haven't seen it. Maybe there are some. But the patient has turned frequently and almost regularly, while he has been suffering, against the group with his mouth or his tongue. And you may say that a gun is more dangerous than a tongue, but not necessarily so. A tongue may be very offensive and therefore dangerous to the individual himself...what he says may cause offense and may antagonize the people he talks to and then again rebound to his disadvantage. The impulse that he thought will serve him is a boomerang and harms because the impulse, if expressed, offends those around the patient." (MFMA, p. 167-168)

NATURE

"Even if you have been a nervous patient for thirty and thirty-five and forty years-and I have seen them-even then, once you learn how to relax and to throw off fears, nature is certain to repair the complication." (MFMA, p. 16)

"Our method is built on the principle that in minor complications like nervous symptoms-even if they are severe they are only minor complications-in minor complications you must set your will against fate, and once you set your will against fate, you relax, and nature has then an opportunity to correct the complication because our body, this means nature, is a self-repairing machine." (MFMA, p 17)

"Trust the power of nature within you to bring about the balance in your life. The body, left to itself, is self-healing. You don't know how to digest an egg. Nobody knows. But your stomach does. If you leave it alone, it will do it for you." (MDO, p. 228)

"In life it is so arranged, or it should be so arranged, that the group feelings overbalance the individualistic feelings without eliminating them. The individualistic feelings are our nature, and they should not be eliminated because they can't be eliminated. They are our nature, and you can't eliminate nature. But they should be kept under control. This means the group feelings and group entities should have a preponderance over the individualistic entities. The group feelings, in other words, should just overbalance the individual feelings, but the individualistic feelings must remain. You can't eradicate them. You can't throw them out of your body. They remain with you from birth to the grave. There is nothing to be done about nature except to control it. And that's what you learn here." (MFMA, p. 255-256)

NERVE RESISTANCE

" [My patients] shy away, persistently and doggedly, from the total view that their symptoms are of the average variety although more persistent in duration and more resistant to management." (MHTWT, p. 212-213)

"There are very few people that have good resistance all around... you are perfectly average compared to patients who have just as little resistance as you have but in another system." (MFMA, p. 19)

"The patient…feels ashamed of the fact that his nervous system is weak. This is…vanity. That patient is vain enough to expect that all his systems must be perfect. I have yet to see a human being that has nothing but perfect systems." (MFMA, p. 33)

"If I want to cure a patient, I have to see to it that I make the patient develop better resistance in his nerve-muscle mechanism. Nerves and muscles go together. I must get the patient to be able to undergo severe tenseness all day, perhaps, but not develop symptoms-then the patient is cured-or to develop only minor symptoms, which is the same thing, reminders perhaps of symptoms. In order to do that, I must do something with the brain of the patient." (MFMA, p. 382)

"It [the impulse] always comes by Fate. I get such impulses, much more dreadful impulses. But my nerves have been steeled and trained to develop resistance, and when dreadful and mischievous and lascivious and blasphemous impulses reach my brain, I look away and wait and they will depart. And they depart in no time because my resistance has been strengthened and Fate is not strong enough to break my resistance once it is strengthened through training." (MDO, p. 144)

"Now let me tell you, when you develop a poor resistance in your nervous system, whether you develop it or whether it is born with you does not matter, but if you have a poor resistance, that was done by fate. You simply don't know yourself, how to arrange it that you create a poor resistance…You did not want to have poor resistance, by no means. And so all of you, when you had your first symptoms, or your first break, or your first decline in nervous reactions, you had it as a heritage from fate. You were not responsible for what happened to you." (MFMA, p. 12-13)

NERVOUS PERSON/NERVOUS PATIENT

"A nervous person is nervous, and that means that every once in a while his organs don't function as they should. There come at times headaches, and sometimes the headaches come in bouts, not merely gradually rising and then declining, but erupting, exploding. But in an hour, in a day, perhaps, they are gone. And now the nervous system can relax, and the person is no longer harassed by nervous disturbances. He is his average self again, and, if he is, then he can function as an average human being...With nervous patients, that's entirely different. Nervous patients may have bouts of symptoms, but, when they recede, they are still there. The bout is gone but not the symptom. The symptom works now on a lower level. It's no longer acute, no longer explosive, no longer working at a peak level, but it is still there. The fatigue was, during the bout, an exhaustion, and now it falls back to the level of a fatigue. But the fatigue is there practically all day, every day, for weeks, for months, and sometimes for years." (MFMA, p. 208-209)

"There are very few people living in this world-in this modern world which has endless strain and stress-there are very few people these days, living in a complex society as we do, that are not nervous persons, very few people." (MFMA, p. 228)

OBJECTIVITY

"There are subjective facts that the subject feels and objective facts that everybody who has eyes, ears, hands, and certain intelligence can verify. And so the title of that article should read, 'Feelings Are Subjective Facts but Not Objective Facts.' But that title would take up about two lines in the book, and we don't want that. Therefore, we merely let it read, 'Feelings Are Not Facts.' But you should supplement in your mind the adjective *objective* and say, 'Feelings Are Not Objective Facts.' " (MFMA, p. 78)

"Emotions are values, and I do not think of inveighing against them, except in regard to nervous patients and nervous symptoms... if you are seized, as is the case in a panic, with the frustrating emotions of fear, anger and despair, with jealousy and envy, with indignation and disgust, then you must bend all your energies to becoming and remaining cool, chilly, unemotional and objective." (MHTWT, p. 128-129)

OBSESSIONS

"My patients are asked to use their muscles primarily for the control of sensations, and more so yet, perhaps, for the control of obsessions and compulsions." (MFMA, p. 313)

"Patients without number have assured me that they 'try and try' to get rid of a disturbing idea but 'it just doesn't work.' My standard reply to remarks of this kind is that if I try to shake off an upsetting or ugly thought I invariably fail, no matter how hard I may 'try and try' until I recognize that I don't know how to do it and give up the futile effort. To forget means to let a memory die away, to permit it to drop out of consciousness...the brain knows very well how to do the job of forgetting because it does it continuously." (Selections, p. 73)

"Patients have sometimes frightful obsessions. They have the obsession that they want to do harm to their children, to their mother, to anybody, to riders on the streetcar, to strangers. But it is, of course, particularly painful if these impulses are directed against mother or children or both. And I tell these patients, 'Don't worry. That impulse is not yours. It's a stranger in your brain.' And I am not going to explain that today. I am not going to explain why I tell patients that their impulses-or the impulses of this kind-are not theirs, that they are strangers in the brain. I will only tell you that I could explain it very minutely and directly. These impulses shot into the brain. They were not admitted. They broke in, and nobody has to be ashamed of a burglar. The burglar wasn't called by you. He came. That is fate. And if an idea shoots in your brain and you can't dislodge it, that is fate...And the individual is advised by me to keep calm, not to try to get rid of this intruder, and the intruder will remove itself. That always happens if a patient ignores the obsession. It may take time, but it happens." (MFMA, p. 280-281)

PANIC

"Emotions are values, and I do not think of inveighing against them, except in regard to nervous patients and nervous symptoms... if you are seized, as is the case in a panic, with the frustrating emotions of fear, anger and despair, with jealousy and envy, with indignation and disgust, then you must bend all your energies to becoming and remaining cool, chilly, unemotional and objective." (MHTWT, p. 128-129)

"A panic is a feeling of extreme distress which annexes either the thought of danger or that of harmlessness. The panics experienced by patients are not pure feelings, they are overlaid and modified and taken captive by a thought. If the annexed thought is that of danger a vicious cycle will develop and the panic will be prolonged. If the thought is that of security the panic will be stopped abruptly. If all depends on whether the patient will accept the physician's thought of security or his own thought of danger... The patient is not asked to change his feelings or to discard them or to disavow them. He is merely asked to substitute the physician's thought for his own." (MHTWT, p. 118)

"With a calm brain there is no possibility of a sustained panic." (MHTWT, p. 364)

"My supreme and only duty is to relieve my patients of their agonies. And if their panics and vicious cycles result from their faulty use of the thinking process I shall advise them to throw overboard the rubbish of modern slogans and let me do their thinking in the matter of interpreting and concluding with regard to symptoms." (MHTWT, p. 226)

PARENTING

"What we call *possessive mothers* are certainly mothers that love their children. They would want to take care of their daughter, not of strangers. But along with this love goes this desire to possess the body and the soul, and every act, and every decision of that daughter. And I have seen mothers who don't let their daughters even boil two eggs. They immediately rush up and say, 'Let me do it.' You can't tell me that this is love." (MFMA, p. 80)

"If a father loves his children and constantly teases them so that they really become distracted, or he constantly says *no* when they ask for something, don't tell me that is love. That father may still love the children, but his love is outstripped by something that we call *domination*. He has no respect for the desires of the children. The children have no desire to constantly [be] teased. They have certainly no desire to be constantly treated with *no*, with negativism." (MFMA, p. 80)

"In every such situation where somebody steps in and takes over, he sows distrust. He hurts the feelings of others for the following reason: Everybody must have some important field in which he is permitted to take care of himself, to live without supervision. And that has been called *the urge to self-determination*. And if that urge to self-determination is thwarted, there results the situation where the person who is thwarted feels a fundamental right is denied him. That fundamental right is to use his own judgment, his own vigilance, his own capabilities. And if this right is denied, then there results what I told you already-distrust, resentment, ill feeling and therefore tenseness." (MFMA, p. 234)

PATIENCE

"The poor wretch that falls into my hands is unlucky because from me he can't expect instant relief. I will tell him to wait. You know that. He has to show patience, and the very least thing that the patient wants to show is patience. He wants instant relief or as speedy relief as possible because his suffering is really outrageous… Of course, I don't have to tell you that I give you instant relief very frequently, too. But I pooh-pooh the value of instant relief. That will never cure you." (MFMA, p. 272)

PERFECTIONISM

"To (a perfectionist)…every puny endeavor, each trivial enterprise is a challenge to prove and to maintain his exceptional stature. His life is a perennial test of his singularity and distinction. For him there are no trivialities, no routine performances. He is forever on trial, before his own inner seat of judgement, for his excellence and exceptional ability. He cannot achieve poise, relaxation, spontaneity. He cannot afford to have the COURAGE TO MAKE MISTAKES. A mistake might wipe out his pretense of being superior, important, exceptional. With no margin left for mistakes he is perpetually haunted by the fear of making them." (MHTWT, p. 250)

"We of Recovery have no use for a system which preaches perfection as an ideal to be achieved through the blessings of a machine-regulated existence. If our mortal state of imperfection can only be redeemed through the 'faultless operation' of lifeless machines, well, we are old-fashioned enough to renounce the machine and enjoy our averageness and spontaneity." (MHTWT, p. 252)

"The patients don't drop their desire for perfection, for exceptionality. And why don't they? The reason is simple. People are vain. You and I are vain. Everybody is vain. Do you know what vanity means? Well, I guess you know, but I shall express it in my words. Vanity means I refuse to be like other people. I insist on being better and finer and smarter than other people. I insist on being superior or singular or excellent, and not just average." (MFMA, p. 154)

PRACTICE & TRAINING

"The one and only goal of the patient must be to regain his mental health. In order to achieve it, the goals and whims and wishes of "human nature" must be held down with ruthless determination." (MHTWT, p. 218-219)

"Understanding alone will not help and has not helped any patient that has developed a long-term nervous problem. The only thing that will help the patient is training, persistent training." (MFMA, p. 9-10)

"The training [of the nervous patient] must be very severe-not cruel, don't misunderstand me-severe, unrelenting, continuous for some great space of time." (MFMA, p. 97)

"Those of my patients who are slow in improving suffer from a dual, divided Will. They want to get well but want it to come to them painlessly, without painful practice. They want health, but they do not want the discomfort of practicing rules and techniques. This means that they want and do not want." (Selections, p. 96)

"Knowledge is good and indispensable for action and planning. But with all the knowledge of the good you will bungle and slip and frequently do the bad. The reason is that after you have learned and know the good you must practice and practice and practice again what you know. It is practice that gives you the skill, the assurance and mastery for correct action." (Selections, p. 118)

"Knowledge teaches you *what* to do, but practice tells you *how* to do it. This goes for ordinary performances, but also for such complex conduct as the art of acting average, the skill in avoiding self-diagnosis and holding down temper. All the theoretical knowledge you may have about them will avail you little unless you add practical training – in self-control. And one of the great accomplishments of our Recovery techniques has been to deflate the value of knowledge and to emphasize the supreme importance of training, and continuous training at that. The continuous training, guided by continuous spotting, yields what we will call: self-management and self-control, both of which combine to furnish self-help." (Selections, p. 118-119)

"What we physicians are able to furnish is knowledge of the problems involved in the subject of domestic temper. The thing that you are required to supply is the determination to practice until control is accomplished. If after a few brief trials you decide that knowledge does not seem to help you, you limited yourself to the one part of our program (the acquisition of insight) but neglected to carry out the other part (the persistent practice based on the newly achieved insight)." (P v. P, p. 124)

"Beliefs are frequently stubborn and obstinate...Muscles are just as likely to develop obstinacy. They tend to acquire set patterns of behavior preferring certain well grooved acts and avoiding others. Just think of the habits of procrastination, of twitches and spasms, of restlessness and sluggishness, and you will realize that muscles are not always pliant tools in the hands of the Will. In order to pry loose the resisting beliefs and rebellious muscles attempt after attempt must be made to dislodge them from their comfortable berth and to force them to give up resistance. The resistance may be so strong that the attempts to break it must be repeated in innumerable trials before success is achieved. This requires the Will to use a great deal of power in continued strenuous practice." (MHTWT, p. 141-142)

"My patients will have to realize what former generations always knew: that a life task can be mastered only through a grueling, exacting learning process in which all the resources of the Will must combine to achieve final fulfillment. Health is a task of this kind. It can be secured only if the patient's Will initiates a system of ceaseless trials and trials and trials until in the end the task is accomplished. If this is done even the most stubborn belief will yield to the influence of the learning process and the most sluggish muscle will obey the dictates of the Will." (MHTWT, p. 144)

"I do not want my patients to believe that cures and remedies must necessarily be complex, involved and time-consuming. It is easy to sit in a chair and be given lengthy and interesting explanations about how fears arise and develop. That is complex but easy. But if a boy is afraid of swimming or diving it is not at all easy to make him move his muscles for the purpose of a resolute jump. That jump is simple but difficult...What will the most lucid explanations profit you if you are seized with a deep anxiety or a paralyzing panic? In a condition of this kind you are utterly unable to make use of the ingenious and fascinating explanations you may have been given." (MHTWT, p. 364-365)

"The notion that by some trick information can change action and direct impulses has gripped the imagination of the age. We in Recovery refuse to believe in magic, and if we want to change our action we devise proper counter-action, and if our impulses need controlling we provide for adequate means of checking them. Our method is that of patient practice supervised by a leader. In our old-fashioned scheme, information is merely the preliminary to training and practice, not a substitute for leadership." (MHTWT, p. 238-239)

"Having lost control over the functions of the nervous system the patient consults the physician asking him to supply the leadership that he himself can no longer provide. Physician and patient are now forming a partnership in which a unified purpose is set and defined by the physician and accepted by the patient. In this partnership the physician represents the group purpose of mental health and self-discipline. The patient accepts it and pledges himself to employ all the necessary means to attain the end." (MHTWT, p. 281-282)

"Once the physician has made the diagnosis of a nervous ailment a goal is set for the patient to aim at…The goal is that of self-discipline. What must be disciplined is the patient's behavior, particularly his behavior toward his inner experiences." (MHTWT, p. 295)

"Many things in a nervous patient are depressed and crowded out of the stream of life. They are in life but don't 'stream.' And in order to make the stream flow again, the stream of feeling, the stream of interest, the stream of mental reaction and emotional reaction, what is required is for the patient not to discourage himself. And in order not to discourage himself, the patient must be trained, trained to develop courage, trained to develop the capacity for braving discomfort-even if you call it torture, but it's still discomfort. And once you learn that, after due training, there is no difficulty to have both validity and vitality restored to its former function, which is then as lively as it ever was." (MFMA, p. 68-69)

"If somebody wishes to master a method he will have to begin his practice where the application is easiest. Suppose you wish to become an airplane pilot. You will first work on prints and models, then on parts, then on machines of simple design and only in the last stage of your apprenticeship will you venture to manipulate the more powerful engines. This gradual progression from relatively simple to increasingly more complex tasks is the system by means of which every method is learned." (MHTWT, p. 381)

"It [the impulse] always comes by Fate. I get such impulses, much more dreadful impulses. But my nerves have been steeled and trained to develop resistance, and when dreadful and mischievous and lascivious and blasphemous impulses reach my brain, I look away and wait and they will depart. And they depart in no time because my resistance has been strengthened and Fate is not strong enough to break my resistance once it is strengthened through training." (MDO, p. 144)

"When you have palpitations, it's very easy and no effort whatever to run to the phone and call the doctor. That's easy. That's comfort, or the prospect of comfort. Here in this organization you are trained to stand discomfort and to make a strenuous effort. And a supreme effort for a nervous patient is to stand his symptoms, not to run to the phone to call the physician, and it's remarkable what you do when you decide to stand the discomfort of the symptom." (MFMA, p. 5)

"How are you going to acquire this knowledge that there is no danger?...Briefly, I'll tell you, such a certain knowledge can only be acquired if you practice it and listen to it and think about it continually till it is settled." (MFMA, p. 9)

"In Recovery you are told that if you want to get well, you have to influence your internal environment-your internal environment that consists mainly of impulses, sensations, obsessions, that must be controlled as you learn here. And, second, of your beliefs, that must be changed according to the standards that you are taught here." (MFMA, p. 56)

"An apprentice is naturally unschooled as a rule when he begins his apprenticeship...What would happen to our workers-to our craftsmen-if, when they begin their apprenticeship, they should become discouraged the first day? We would have no craftsmen. And yet that is what our patients do. They have a passion to be discouraged, and that means they don't consider themselves apprentices." (MFMA, p. 59)

"The training process in Recovery...consists in a simple phrase, in making the patient realize that he is in apprenticeship." (MFMA, p. 60)

"I hope that you will go home now-after having some refreshments, of course-and will give some thought to what you have heard me say. And if you do, don't expect that from now on you will change, even if you give careful thought to what I have told you and what is only a repetition of what I used to tell you and have told you so many times...Once you make up your mind you want to change, in order to change, you must undergo training, and that takes time. And please don't become disappointed if you make up your mind today to use your sense of humor, and you find out that tomorrow that you have not used it. Well, that's perfectly average and human." (MFMA, p. 100)

"Whatever is conscious is at the surface of thinking. And anybody can understand and, at the same time, explain the surface appearances of the mind, but the surface only. Everything else requires laborious training. If you want to go down to the depths of meanings, both with regard to statements or reactions, you have to make a special study. The study will require you to learn the techniques of spotting." (MFMA, p. 204)

"Poor habits can be acquired in a fraction of a second, good habits only in long, protracted training." (MFMA, p. 216)

"I deal with patients, and therefore I am, of course, partial to the notion of training. How can a patient get well unless he establishes the habit of control of his impulses, control of his temper, control of his keen desire to make his own diagnosis, control of his desire to constantly check his body and find out the spots that he thinks are decaying or rotting? If I don't establish new habits in him, then how can he get well? How can he acquire, then, the habits that he needs?" (MFMA, p. 217-218)

REALISM

"Recovery stands for realism, plain common sense and an unspoiled way of viewing life." (MFMA, p. 65)

"If a person expects to live in a world purged of frustrations and obstructions, his extravagant *expectations* will of necessity invite *disappointments*. Then tempers will rise abundantly, and symptoms will not go down rapidly." (Selections, p. 129)

"Spontaneity means that you are not self-conscious, that you are not on your guard for fear of making mistakes. Spontaneity means the COURAGE TO MAKE MISTAKES. In trivial or routine activities no calamity arises if perchance a mistake occurs. This is the reason why realists, that is, men and women of average aspirations go about their daily tasks with due caution and circumspection, it is true, but without any marked fear of making a mistake. Mistakes made in trivial performances are trivial themselves and their possible consequences are just as trivial and not to be feared. With the fear of mistakes largely removed from the mind of the realist his decisions are reached with ease and his actions initiated without undue hesitation. All of this is the result of spontaneity and, in turn, favors its development." (MHTWT, p. 249-250)

REVIEW/PREVIEW

"When my patients begin to lash out against themselves, to accuse themselves, to condemn themselves, they do something that gives the self-condemnation duration...they think of how they acted previously...When I look back into my past, I could easily exclaim, 'Oh, what a rascal have I been!' Well, what of it? So, I have been a rascal numerous times... I am an average person. I am like everybody is." (MFMA, p. 42-43)

"Patients who suffer from a depression think that whatever they do is wrong. They think whatever they have done in the past is wrong, and they recount past misdemeanors and so-called delinquencies, which have perhaps some basis in fact but are monstrously exaggerated. And you understand that such patients categorically deny that there is anything right in their thinking." (MFMA, p. 66)

RIGHT VS. WRONG

"The wildest temper outburst can be checked instantly if you take the objective attitude that you are not the judge as to who is right or wrong." (MHTWT, p. 127)

"Patients who suffer from a depression think that whatever they do is wrong. They think whatever they have done in the past is wrong, and they recount past misdemeanors and so-called delinquencies, which have perhaps some basis in fact but are monstrously exaggerated. And you understand that such patients categorically deny that there is anything right in their thinking." (MFMA, p. 66)

"Whether you are right or wrong is immaterial. Temper is a matter of breeding, not of right and wrong." (Lost and Found, Vol. 2, No. 4, 1939 reprinted in Recovery Reporter, Vol. 63, No. 2, March-April 2000)

"This assurance of oneself being right and the other person wrong is the essential basis of what I described as the domestic attitude of the problem adult. It is the rock on which most unsuccessful marital relations are currently wrecked." (P v. P, p. 52)

"Mark it: whenever you do not know whether you are right or wrong you are bound to be tense." (P v. P, p. 75)

"Forever afraid of being wrong, a conflict-torn or dilemma-plagued individual is anxious to convince himself that, in actual fact, he is right…The most effective method of establishing one's claim to being right is a stubborn insistence on being listened to, on getting one's suggestions accepted and one's dictates acted on. This secures a sense of mastery and disposes, for the moment, of the suspicion of one's being 'wrong. Persons embroiled in perpetual inner conflicts are, therefore, eager to gain mastery over the partner. The common tendency to be domineering has here its root. It begins with the sense of being wrong, proceeds to the claim to be right, and ends in the overwhelming desire to dominate each and every situation." (P v. P, p. 78)

"The man of breeding has been trained to secure satisfaction from subduing his own inclination. He scorns the pleasure derived from bullying or imposing on others. Moreover, the man of breeding while desiring to do right is not afraid-in daily trivialities-of being wrong. Hence he has no desire to prove that others are wrong. The result is that he is serene, genial, and conciliatory." (P v. P, p. 83)

"If a man secures from an act the pleasurable feeling of being right he will refuse to abandon it and *choose* to continue. But for the premium of pleasure that rests on temperamental behavior a change of temper would be as easy as a change in clothing. The obvious inference is that in order to make men control their tempers they must be made to realize that the claim to be right is no justification for the will to be rude." (P v. P, p. 90)

"This is the crux of domestic discord in practically all its manifestations: one partner bullies the other and has the unobscured insight that bullying is indefensible. But the insight is without effect because it is swept aside by the self-deception that the bullying is done "by right." Do you see the involved tragedy? Humans are so constituted that they relish a "fight for rights." If they manage to convince themselves that their fight is one for "rights" the prospects are they will be reluctant to cease fighting and will *choose* to continue. The result will be the 'temperamental deadlock'." (P v. P, p. 92)

"There are occasions-rare in civilized groups-when men fight for *objective realities.* There are occasions when they are *really and objectively* assaulted and insulted. There are other occasions when vicious, scheming, unscrupulous persons attempt to gain an unfair advantage over them. Occasions of this kind call for fight. But that fight is, as a rule, fought coolly, deliberately, with slow moves and well-calculated measures. The impulsive outburst, the rise of temper, and sudden attack are, as a rule foreign to such realistic struggles…I wish you would grasp this fundamental distinction: fights for realities are rare in the daily round of average life, and the fights encountered in domestic discord are almost invariably centered around the imaginary issue of 'being right'." (P v. P, p. 93)

"It is the process of rationalization that is most apt to cloud insight and block its operation… Rationalization makes 'right' what insight declares 'wrong' and endorses as socially desirable what insight condemns as socially reprehensible." (P v. P, p. 132)

"I remember many of the evil things I have done, not all. What do I do then? Why do I not sink in the ground with shame? It was an average past. Why should I blame myself for an average past?" (MDO, p. 144)

ROMANTICISM/INTELLECTUALISM

"In point of *inner responses* men are alike. They differ only in their readiness to convert their inner responses into *open reactions*. The realist is inclined to control his feeling and thought responses; the romantic and intellectual tend to express them." (MHTWT, p.76)

"I am little concerned about the political, economic or social views of my patients. What interests me is their philosophy with regard to symptoms and temper. The fact is that my patients, prior to receiving training in Recovery, have been stubbornly romantic about their symptoms and emphatically intellectual about their temper." (MHTWT, p.79)

"It is the distinctive mark of the so-called intellectual to emphasize or over-emphasize one side of an issue only, usually his own side, and to look away from the other side. Much of what I have told you in the past ten years about temper can be safely condensed in the one concise formulation: temper is, among other things, the result of an intellectual blindness to the 'other side of the story.' " (MHTWT, p. 158-159)

"Everybody, not only my patients, has the natural impulse to prove the superiority of his thinking abilities (intellectual validity) and to demonstrate the exquisite quality of his strength, forcefulness and prowess (romantic vitality)." (MHTWT, p. 163-164)

"A person's reasoning is powerfully influenced by the values cultivated in his group. And our contemporary group has placed a preposterous valuation on romanto-intellectual wants to the detriment of realistic needs." (MHTWT, p. 202)

"Whether it is the angry or fearful temper, the situation is the same. The patient 'knows better.' He is an arch romanto-intellectual who knows and is sure and cannot be convinced without a long, drawn-out struggle. If he is to be cured, he must be trained to assume a humble attitude and to divest himself of the vanity of knowing. The road to humility leads through spotting to the determination to abandon the craving for the divine thrill of knowing better." (MHTWT, p. 167)

SABOTAGE

"What the patient resists and sabotages is the physician's knowledge that nervous ailments require Will-training, Self-discipline and Self-control. What he fights for is his own conviction that he needs outside help for an ailment which has nothing to do with Will, discipline or control." (Selections, p. 71)

"If observations are made and conclusions drawn with regard to symptoms the process is called the art of making a diagnosis. That this art is difficult, utterly complex and reserved for thoroughly trained persons only is generally accepted. But my patients ignore what everybody knows and when they observe a symptom they promptly rush to supply a diagnosis of their own…Their theory is that anybody who is not an outright moron knows how to use the thinking process and for a person of 'normal intelligence' it is 'no trick' to make reliable observations and draw valid conclusions. In this, they display an enormous contempt for the complexity of the techniques and rules of solid thinking." (MHTWT, p. 224)

"The concept of sabotage is basic to the philosophy of Recovery. The nervous patient sabotages his own health, his social adjustment, his efficiency and equilibrium and-most pernicious form of sabotage- the physician's authority. The trouble is that the patient, engaged in a systematic effort of obstruction, plies his trade in such a subtle and almost underhanded manner that he is not aware of his own plottings and machinations." (MHTWT, p. 261)

"The patient who opposes the freely selected physician sabotages a self-chosen purpose...He has adopted and accepted the purpose of health and has appointed his physician to help him realize the purpose. If he obstructs the physician's efforts he frustrates his own purpose and, by this token, is a self-saboteur." (MHTWT, p. 271)

SELF-BLAME

"When I think of myself as average, then everything that is average, that is done by people on an average, is permissible and I will not blame myself for doing it." (MFMA, p. 73)

"The patient...feels ashamed of the fact that his nervous system is weak. This is...vanity. That patient is vain enough to expect that all his systems must be perfect. I have yet to see a human being that has nothing but perfect systems." (MFMA, p. 33)

"Stop blaming yourself for your averageness, for your average human imperfection, for human limitations. And if you stop blaming yourself, you will, incidentally, naturally whittle down that thing that you now call, that I ask you to call *the passion for self-distrust*." (MFMA, p. 311)

"Recovery, or any other procedure, can never train you how to change the quality of your feelings or how to call upon certain feelings or how to prevent certain feelings from entering your consciousness. So...don't blame yourself for lacking a feeling, or for possessing another feeling that you don't like to possess." (MFMA, p. 85)

"When my patients begin to lash out against themselves, to accuse themselves, to condemn themselves, they do something that gives the self-condemnation duration…they think of how they acted previously…When I look back into my past, I could easily exclaim, 'Oh, what a rascal have I been!' Well, what of it? So, I have been a rascal numerous times… I am an average person. I am like everybody is." (MFMA, p. 42-43)

"If you have had any reaction that you might be ashamed of, be certain I had it and all humanity had it, except the saints." (MFMA, p. 43)

"I make…mistakes, too, …and then I ask myself, 'what's the matter with me?' And my answer is, 'Well, nothing is the matter with me. I am average.' And that's what average people do." (MFMA, p. 98-99)

"When I have an impulse, be certain I did not summon it. I did not call it into being. I didn't make any effort to get this impulse started, especially if it is an impulse that I hate, that I don't want. Then be certain I am not responsible for it. This means I didn't create it. I didn't do anything to bring it to the fore. So why should I blame myself? Why should I feel disgraced?...And…that's what all of you do." (MFMA, p. 450)

"If you are one of those patients that in the morning feel limp, devitalized, tired, exhausted-and you know I have quite a few of these patients-and then you make up your mind, regardless of how tired you are, how limp you feel, how lifeless you are, regardless of all of this, you will jump out of bed and do things, then you have scored a victory…if a patient does that, he has definitely gained a victory over a formidable enemy, that is, his incapacity. Why is he not proud of himself?" (MFMA, p. 31-32)

"The daily round of the average individual consists, in the main, of such trivial performances as reading, conversing, working on a job, cooking, washing, cleaning, telephoning, shopping…In trivial or routine activities, no calamity arises if perchance a mistake occurs. This is the reason why realists, that is, men and women of average aspirations, go about their daily tasks with due caution and circumspection, it is true, but without any marked fear of making a mistake. Mistakes made in trivial performances are trivial themselves, and their possible consequences are just as trivial and not to be feared." (MHTWT, p. 249)

"If, as some maintain, sex exercises a powerful influence on average daily existence the effect is due to the *thought about sex* rather than to the sexual impulses as such. Aside from the exceptional instances of sex aberrations and sex delinquencies, sex life in itself is not likely to result in abnormal behavior. It produces maladjustment only or mainly if it is linked to such thoughts as sin, guilt, disgrace, self-blame and self-contempt, expectation of punishment and anticipation of dire consequence to health. Again, you see how even here thought dominates feeling." (P v. P, p. 190)

"Spontaneity means that you are not self-conscious, that you are not on your guard for fear of making mistakes. Spontaneity means the COURAGE TO MAKE MISTAKES. In trivial or routine activities no calamity arises if perchance a mistake occurs. This is the reason why realists, that is, men and women of average aspirations go about their daily tasks with due caution and circumspection, it is true, but without any marked fear of making a mistake. Mistakes made in trivial performances are trivial themselves and their possible consequences are just as trivial and not to be feared. With the fear of mistakes largely removed from the mind of the realist his decisions are reached with ease and his actions initiated without undue hesitation. All of this is the result of spontaneity and, in turn, favors its development." (MHTWT, p. 249-250)

"The average person has fears, and headaches, and numbness, and develops a palpitation here and a pressure there, but if he feels average, then he takes it for granted that that is coming to him and therefore doesn't work himself up over it. If he feels average, he will not blame himself for having palpitations, not even for having the feeling that he is dying away. He will simply take it for granted that he is an average human being with the average human limitations." (MFMA, p. 75)

"Errors are the most common occurrence in everybody's experience. Indeed, there would be no sound and tested experience unless errors were made, and made repeatedly and then corrected. It is precisely the correction of errors which gives correct experience. If this is so, then errors are a necessary and desirable and wholesome part of life even if they are repeated three times and dozens of times and hundreds of times." (MHTWT, p. 241)

"I remember many of the evil things I have done, not all. What do I do then? Why do I not sink in the ground with shame? It was an average past. Why should I blame myself for an average past?" (MDO, p. 144)

"Our patients are implacable enemies of themselves. They fear themselves, this means their impulses. They are ashamed of themselves, this means their impulses or actions or feelings. They indeed hate themselves, or, if I am to use a milder term, they resent themselves, but essentially it is self-hatred." (MFMA, p. 95)

SELF-DIAGNOSIS

"Don't listen to anybody who will tell you [that] once you have had a severe nervous or mental condition that you will never come back. That's, of course, arrant nonsense, and don't listen to such prophets of doom." (MFMA, p. 69)

"Such phrases as 'I have to,' 'I can't,' or 'I try my best but can I help it if I don't succeed?' mean that the patient diagnoses his condition as a physical disease in which Fate has paralyzed his Will. No matter how skillfully fitting is the context in which phrases of this kind are used, they mean nothing less than the diagnosis of an organic ailment…the patient refuses to accept the physician's diagnosis of a distressing but harmless nervous disturbance insisting on self-diagnosing it as a serious organic ailment. The tragedy is that self-diagnosing is anything but an innocent pastime. It breeds defeatism and fatalism, continued tenseness and endless agony." (Selections, p. 61)

"I wish that all my patients performed this little experiment on themselves. When they fear that their dizziness or numbness will lead them to destruction, I wish they would ask themselves the question: If Mr. X had my dizziness or numbness and feared they will kill or cripple him, would I believe that? If you ask this question all the time you might be well all the time." (Selections, p. 127)

"What the patient resists and sabotages is the physician's knowledge that nervous ailments require Will-training, Self-discipline and Self-control. What he fights for is his own conviction that he needs outside help for an ailment which has nothing to do with Will, discipline or control." (Selections, p. 71)

"In my more than thirty years of intensive experience with patients I have met nothing but average cases. In all of them I have observed the following pattern: There are the average run of symptoms which are due to average type of tenseness, and the tenseness is created or maintained by either temper or self-diagnosing or by both. And the average patient can easily discover within himself both temper and self-diagnosing." (Selections, p. 109)

"I have not seen a patient who was not helpless, totally or partially. Patients are helpless to stop their pressures, they are helpless when they find themselves seized with air-hunger or night terror. And if any patient claims to be helpless I shall not challenge the correctness of his statement. But when a patient declares himself hopeless I shall warn him that he has presumed to make a prognosis and has trespassed into my territory. The physician alone is capable of deciding whether a condition is hopeless or hopeful." (MHTWT, p. 96)

"Spotting means for you to be perpetually on guard against your inveterate tendency to 'do your own thinking' when observing a symptom and its accompanying temperamental reaction. It means a ruthless determination to eliminate self-diagnosing and thus to do away with panics, vicious cycles and endless horrors of agony." (MHTWT, p. 227)

"Let me tell you that this excuse that 'I have had weak nerves all my life' does not count a thing in point of curability. Every nervous condition can be cured, regardless of its duration-by the way, also regardless of its intensity." (MFMA, p. 367)

"Once you call your condition a condition that can't be helped-this means that it is either untreatable or incurable-well, then you naturally develop a scare, alarm; you become hopeless, and you work up tenseness...And those of you that are regular customers here know that to cut out tenseness means don't make a disastrous diagnosis. Don't diagnose insecurity, incurability, untreatability. Diagnose as I have done. Accept as I have done." (MFMA, p. 370)

"Whenever a patient makes for his symptoms these strict distinctions of having a dizziness on the street but never, or seldom, at home, then you will understand that such a symptom cannot come from a damaged organ. And whenever you have such a distinction, then you could be sure that this is nervous. Only the brain can make such a distinction, not the heart, damaged or undamaged. It's good for you to know that." (MFMA, p. 458)

"If observations are made and conclusions drawn with regard to symptoms the process is called the art of making a diagnosis. That this art is difficult, utterly complex and reserved for thoroughly trained persons only is generally accepted. But my patients ignore what everybody knows and when they observe a symptom they promptly rush to supply a diagnosis of their own...Their theory is that anybody who is not an outright moron knows how to use the thinking process and for a person of 'normal intelligence' it is 'no trick' to make reliable observations and draw valid conclusions. In this, they display an enormous contempt for the complexity of the techniques and rules of solid thinking." (MHTWT, p. 224)

"A woman had been suffering from fatigue, poor sleep, headaches, dizziness, chest pressure and all kinds of other threatening sensations. Most annoying was a sensation felt in the abdomen of churning and tremulousness which was present all day every day...All tests were negative, and the diagnosis was invariably that of a nervous condition. She was seen in the fourth year of her invalidism and made considerable headway in response to private interviews and class treatment. Nevertheless, she insisted that the constant churning must have a 'cause.' This term 'cause' is frequently mentioned by patients who resent having their disturbance classified as nervous. Nervousness, to them, means a condition for which there is no 'cause.' It means a trouble which has to do with lack of will-power, self-pampering, refusal to get well, in short, poor morale and weak character. The 'cause,' if found, would instantly redeem the moral status of the patient, and the stigma of low morale would fall to the ground." (MHTWT, p. 297)

"A rather common attempt to reject the diagnosis of a nervous ailment is the recourse to heredity…There is certainly no glory in a hereditary ailment. There can be scant consolation in the thought that one's ancestors were 'tainted.' But anything sounds more hopeful and more comforting than the bleak prospect of having to undergo training in self-discipline. Even brain tumors, mental ailments and hereditary 'taints' are preferable to that dreadful indictment as being a weak character and needing training in self-control." (MHTWT, p. 299)

"I will advise you, don't go on constantly discouraging yourselves by thinking that your vitality is gone and dead. It is merely dormant. It hibernates. It is not active. And now you can activate it or reactivate it [if you stop maintaining] the idea that anything in your body is dead. Nature works differently. There is nothing dead in the body if you are alive. The only things that are half dead are such structures as hair and nails, but everything else is alive. But it may be dormant, it may be asleep, inactive." (MFMA, p. 68)

"A diagnosis must naturally not be based on feelings. It must be based on objective facts that can be diagnosed, for instance, by tests, by examinations, by x-rays, by all kinds of evidence that only the physician can supply and which the physician only can interpret." (MFMA, p. 79)

"Nervous fatigue is a condition that has its highest intensity in the morning, dwindling in strength in the afternoon and disappearing in the evening…Now if your muscles were weak to the point of exhaustion why should they regain their strength after a day's exertion. This alone ought to convince you that your fatigue is a feeling and nothing else." (MHTWT, p. 383-384)

"Accept my diagnosis. I have the experience, of course, with thousands of conditions and patients. You have the experience with your own case. That's no experience. That is the experience of one case. And even if you say that you have a very close and intimate knowledge of your case, I grant you, you have. You have the knowledge that I don't have. I don't know whether your heart is now palpitating, whether your stomach is tightening up right now. I don't know that. You know, but do you understand what that means? Do you understand whether that means danger or security? You feel what you feel inside, but you don't know what it means. It is only the diagnosis, made by a competent and experienced man, that gives the meaning to your suffering, and that's, of course, very important. If I [know] what your condition signifies, then I can pick the correct treatment according to my experience, which is seasoned." (MFMA, p. 132)

"Here in Recovery we have finally made it clear to the patients-and sometimes we have made it clear to the world-that even if a patient has reached that final stage that is largely featured in the textbooks, we are not afraid of it. And therefore we go ahead, take care of these patients, restore them to health in a great number of instances. And, as a further consequence, we have therefore adopted the slogan, 'There are no hopeless cases among nervous patients, regardless of the final duration of the condition.'" (MFMA, p. 211)

"For the patient it is of the utmost importance to know how to interpret his inner life and what conclusions to reach. And that's what the patient is trained to do in Recovery. In Recovery he has, with regard to his health, to use his physician's interpretations only-with regard to health I say-and the physician's conclusions only. And if he fails to do that, then he makes his own interpretations and his own conclusions at his own risk, and the risk is formidable. The risk means sustained tenseness, endless strains and trains of symptoms, and vicious cycles and panics." (MFMA, p. 257)

SELF-DISCIPLINE

"Once the physician has made the diagnosis of a nervous ailment a goal is set for the patient to aim at…The goal is that of self-discipline. What must be disciplined is the patient's behavior, particularly his behavior toward his inner experiences." (MHTWT, p. 295)

"A rather common attempt to reject the diagnosis of a nervous ailment is the recourse to heredity…There is certainly no glory in a hereditary ailment. There can be scant consolation in the thought that one's ancestors were 'tainted.' But anything sounds more hopeful and more comforting than the bleak prospect of having to undergo training in self-discipline. Even brain tumors, mental ailments and hereditary 'taints' are preferable to that dreadful indictment as being a weak character and needing training in self-control." (MHTWT, p. 299)

SELF-DISTRUST

"Stop blaming yourself for your averageness, for your average human imperfection, for human limitations. And if you stop blaming yourself, you will, incidentally, naturally whittle down that thing that you now call, that I ask you to call *the passion for self-distrust*." (MFMA, p. 311)

"Nervousness and nervous symptoms are universal and average and…to get well means to become again an average nervous person who experiences nervous reactions in many phases of his life but has implicit confidence in the trustworthiness of his basic functions." (Selections, p. 10)

"If, after due examination, I tell a patient that his is a nervous ailment, the implication is that his physical and mental tools are in good condition and that the only thing wrong with him is his mental attitude of self-distrust…To cure a nervous patient means to change his mental attitude, that is, to make him drop his romanticisms and intellectualisms and to substitute a realistic outlook. If this is accomplished, a mental attitude of self-trust is installed, and the physical and mental tools of the body can then aim straight at their goals, without fear, without self-consciousness, without morbid preoccupation." (Selections, p. 48)

"My daily life is crowded with occasions in which I fumble and falter. While walking on the street I sometimes stumble or bump into another person. Occasionally I slip or fall on the wet or icy sidewalk. At times I actually hurt myself. Nevertheless, I do not conceive a violent distrust of my Self but consider the misstep or mishap as part of my life. The same holds true for numerous other experiences of my daily round. It happens frequently that I talk to people and fear I said too much. Or, I feel I did not say enough or said the wrong thing. Or, I fall into the trap of a slick salesman who, taking advantage of my preoccupation, tricks me into an ill-considered purchase. In all these instances my Self, physical or social, fails me but I do not lose trust in it." (MHTWT, p. 242)

"To have trust in one's organs and functions is to be spontaneous. Spontaneity means…, for instance, that you have an intention and your muscles carry it out, promptly, without hesitation, with precision and determination." (MHTWT, p. 243)

"My patients are paralyzed by the fear of making mistakes. They are just as good-and in many instances much better-than the average person, but they are afraid to make mistakes." (MFMA, p. 60)

"Any distrust that you create within you against somebody else, but more so against yourself, will create tenseness. And as long as this self-distrust is maintained, the tenseness will stay with you. It will endure. It will gain duration. And that's the principal characteristic of the nervous patient: that he is likely to produce what other people don't have to produce, and this is enduring tenseness, because he is enduringly disturbed now by his self-distrust." (MFMA, p. 264)

SELF-HELP

"Self-Help as practiced in Recovery is not merely a vague and shadowy theory but a concrete and living reality." (Selections, p. 32)

"My patients come to me, and they think I neglect certain aspects of their suffering, that I don't understand what they actually need. I ask them to get well through self-control, but the patient thinks, and some of them tell me, 'Well, why are you my doctor if I have to help myself? Can't you help me?' Patients have told me that. That's an unfair statement. There is no doubt that if I ask a patient to exercise self-control, self-discipline, and to help himself, that does by no means [mean] that I am not ready to do my part in helping him." (MFMA, p. 27)

"And now you know that this is our ultimate goal, to make the patients help themselves. I don't have to tell you, I hope, that that again requires time and waiting. And if any one of you doesn't want to spend the time and doesn't want to wait, well, let me merely say I hope you will finally find your rest and peace without waiting, without spending time. But I am afraid that is a very pious wish, and you know pious wishes usually do not materialize." (MFMA, p. 275)

SELF-IMPORTANCE

"The supreme task of the nervous patient is to avoid symptoms and temper and...both symptoms and temper are easily aroused by the insistence on being treated as important." (Selections, p. 21)

"A hurt to one's self-importance is nothing more than a shock to one's personal vanity...the sense of personal importance is nothing but an idle claim and silly pretense, and the best thing that can happen to it is to be hurt every once in a while. The occasional hurt will offer a welcome opportunity to practice spotting of vanities, shallowness and conceit." (Selections, p. 50)

"The common frustrations of daily life can be borne and remedied by a sense of humor. It takes a sense of humor to think of one's self and one's frustrations as average. The philosophy of Recovery is opposed to the sense of self-importance and favors the sense of group-importance. The knowledge that 'I am not so important' creates a sense of humor." (Selections, p. 110)

"To be able to laugh at a thing means to refuse to take it seriously. The trouble with the ill-bred individual is that he takes his stirrings, his conflicts, and fears ridiculously seriously. The well-bred person has a sense of humor; the ill-mannered person lacks it." (P v. P, p. 84)

"Everybody has illusions and in order to save them refuses to see facts which are apt to destroy or weaken them. The most common illusion is that of one's own 'self' being important. Daily occurrences demonstrate to everybody how relatively unimportant is his 'self.'...Nevertheless, the illusion of self-importance is maintained against the evidence of facts. Should the facts and their evidence be looked at, the individual would discover his shortcomings and gain insight into his basic weakness. The insight would be shocking and disillusioning. In order to forestall the shock of disillusionment the individual silences the voice of insight and blocks its function." (P v. P, p. 166)

"To a certain extent, the sense of importance is a desirable quality because it is the basis of self-confidence and self-respect. Unfortunately, many people confuse importance with superiority." (P v. P, p. 167)

"I have an egregious sense of importance...it always comes up. I always feel, 'I am the smartest, the finest, the most vital person there is,' but I don't believe it." (MDO, p. 143)

"The sense of shame, of fear, of hatred, of contempt applied to trivialities of life have this in common: that they are utterly out of the range of humor. A person hating trivialities, fearing trivialities, being ashamed of daily trivialities, has, of course, no sense of humor. And my patients, as long as they are suffering from their panics, from their frightful sensations and impulses, and so forth, have, of course, no sense of humor. They take their inner experiences too seriously." (MFMA, p. 96-97)

"Do you understand now that having a good sense of humor and feeling average are the same thing? And looking on his troubles with a great sense of importance is the same thing as having no sense of humor. So, this matter of importance is opposed to the matter of averageness, and the sense of humor is opposed, naturally, to the sense of importance." (MFMA, p. 99)

"You want to be superior. This means you depend on others to either recognize you, to give you credit as being not just average, to give you the honor of constantly catering to you, perhaps do you the favor of constantly flattering you. And if you don't get credit and if you don't get honor and if you don't get flattery, then you become tense because you expect it and you don't get it. And therefore vanity and the striving for perfection is harmful, particularly to the nervous patient. Because since vanity is usually not accomplished, since being vain you don't get people to give you the due credit and flattery and honor, therefore you become tense. Vanity always makes you tense. And if you are a nervous patient, and your vanity makes you tense, the tenseness creates symptoms, and you can't get well. At least you can't get well quickly, in due time." (MFMA, p. 155)

"The self protrudes itself into every situation. And in that situation in which I find myself so frequently every day, and sometimes almost all day, that I am confronted with a patient or with a group of patients, you may think that in my mind there is then practically nothing than the patient's interest, the patient's concerns, and not my self-concern. But that is not so. I have something that we call self-importance, the sense of self-importance." (MFMA, p. 252)

"The nervous patient is allergic to tenseness, to the tenseness of the kind that derives from temper particularly. And if your individualistic feeling of importance is bruised or hurt, and you become angry, then you develop tenseness, temperamental tenseness, and that produces symptoms." (MFMA, p. 255)

"All your feelings, including your feelings about your symptoms, which are thoroughly individualistic, should be held down. They should be controlled. You should not pamper them, and coddle them, and not constantly think of them as being so dangerous and so overpowering. And that's what we call in Recovery *controlling your self-importance.*" (MFMA, p. 256)

"Let me tell you, the setbacks to which a nervous patient is liable are mainly caused by the renewed tenseness that comes from a renewed temper, which stems from the renewed importance that you give yourself-again, self-importance. And if you have learned the distinction between self-importance and group importance in relation to tenseness and symptoms, well, then you have indeed learned a great deal." (MFMA, p. 256)

SELF-LEADERSHIP

"If you make any reasonable effort [to apply the Recovery Method], then you are not responsible whether the effort is successful or not. But you must make an effort." (MFMA, p. 13)

"If a patient improves and adds more improvement as he goes along the route of recovery, and a little improvement again and again, although he does not reach the goal of health quickly, but if he improves measurably, then I know he has done his part." (MFMA, p. 13)

"Muscles always carry out orders that are meant-orders which are resolutely passed on to them." (MHTWT, p. 333)

"The fundamental principle of Recovery [is] that symptoms can be conquered by means of simple and innocent procedures initiated by the patient, i.e., through self-help." (MHTWT, p. 126)

"Without decisions, plans, action and initiative, there is no possibility of developing pride, self-reliance and self-sufficiency." (MHTWT, p. 42)

"There is no task that can be performed on the spot if the task is significant. And where is there a task that is more significant than to restore your health?...And that requires time...it must require particularly much time because we don't want you always to depend on leadership, but finally you must learn to establish self-leadership. And that's what we call *self-help*." (MFMA, p. 275)

"Emotions function as a team with intellect as their manager. There are many emotions but there should be one intellect only. This means that intellect must not be *divided* by several conflicting thoughts but must be *determined* by one leading idea. Intellect, as the team manager, determines which member of the emotional team should, at a given moment, be accorded the privilege to release a corresponding act of behavior, and which are to be restrained. If intellect displays managing ability the emotional team will be well balanced." (P v. P, p. 36-37)

"If you are one of those patients that in the morning feel limp, devitalized, tired, exhausted-and you know I have quite a few of these patients-and then you make up your mind, regardless of how tired you are, how limp you feel, how lifeless you are, regardless of all of this, you will jump out of bed and do things, then you have scored a victory...if a patient does that, he has definitely gained a victory over a formidable enemy, that is, his incapacity. Why is he not proud of himself?" (MFMA, p. 31-32)

"What Annette learned in Recovery and what all my patients are expected to learn there is to approach things with a proper set of valuations. It is your table of valuations which tells you what is important or trivial, what is essential and what insignificant...A thing is valuable if it promotes inner peace leading to contentment, well-being and self-respect; or, if it advances the cause of outer peace resulting in adjustment to family, friends, neighbors, co-workers. If your main aim is to secure peace you are a realist. Then, the attainment of inner and outer peace is your supreme value." (MHTWT, p. 198-199)

"The notion that by some trick information can change action and direct impulses has gripped the imagination of the age. We in Recovery refuse to believe in magic, and if we want to change our action we devise proper counter-action, and if our impulses need controlling we provide for adequate means of checking them. Our method is that of patient practice supervised by a leader. In our old-fashioned scheme, information is merely the preliminary to training and practice, not a substitute for leadership." (MHTWT, p. 238-239)

"In the adult person who has achieved maturity one group purpose, usually that of the family, is expected to *take the lead* over all other purposes and to guide action towards unified behavior. The dominant group purpose supplies *leadership*. Every purpose which conflicts with the leading group purpose must be checked and prevented from exerting itself. In this manner the natural conflict of purposes is controlled. If leadership is not established two antagonistic purposes act against one another producing the condition known as *cross-purpose or dual purpose*. An individual possessed of a unified purpose is said to represent an *integrated* personality. He is endowed with the qualities of leadership." (MHTWT, p. 280-281)

"The patient suffering from a nervous ailment may be and frequently is an integrated personality with regard to the purposes of family, citizenship and vocation. But with regard to his own body he has lost leadership. His impulses, sensations, feelings and thoughts embark on action independent of his dominant purpose." (MHTWT, p. 281)

"I want you to distinguish clearly and energetically between the event that happens in environment, either in outer environment or in inner environment, and the attitude which you take-not the event, but you. The attitude is yours. It is not of the event. And if you bungle, it's due to your attitude, and the attitude can be controlled, can be changed, can be improved. It can be omitted, it can be adopted, it can be manipulated. The event usually cannot." (MFMA, p. 108)

"The patient has to be a leader to himself, and that's very difficult to be." (MFMA, p. 116)

"An average person can have fears and go ahead and act his life regardless of the fear. And that's what you are trained to do in Recovery. In Recovery, we tell you everything that you suffer from – fears, angers, anxieties, pains, pressures – it's all average. And all of these are happenings, accidents, chance events. But now you must exercise something that is not chance but choice, not accident but intention, and that is the will. Have the will to go through your fears and angers and pressures like an average person does or is expected to do. And if you do that, then you will have carried out the main principle of the training which we give here, and, in addition, you will get well." (MFMA, p. 160)

"It's difficult to know what comfort is permissible and what effort is dispensable. And when the patient, for instance, wants some comfort, why shouldn't he get it? And he should get it if it can be provided. But if it interferes with a duty and obligation, for instance, the duty to get well, then I would advise the patient not to look for comfort and rather to make an effort to reach the goal of health." (MFMA, p. 274)

"Inside you there must be leadership. And if there is solid leadership inside you, then forget about your duality. Then you are unified. There is one leader. And if you are subject to one leader, if you have established one principle within you as leader, then you don't have to become alarmed about the waywardness of you inner experiences, or of some of them." (MFMA, p. 280)

SENSATIONS

"If a person is seized with grief or stimulated by joy it would be senseless for the Will to claim that the joy is false or the grief impossible. Feelings are either experienced or not experienced. Their existence, wisdom and probability cannot be denied or affirmed. The same holds for sensations. If the head aches it would be absurd for the Will to object that, 'No, this is no headache. It is unwise, untrue or improbable.' Clearly, if the Will is to intervene in order to control the total experience of insecurity its 'no' cannot be directed to feelings and sensations. Instead, it must address itself to thoughts and impulses." (MHTWT, p. 137)

"Sensations and feelings rise and fall provided you do not attach the idea of danger at the moment the curve reaches its peak." (MHTWT, p. 356)

"I am not primarily interested in temper as a disturbance of social relations. I am interested in it mainly because it maintains and intensifies nervous symptoms. This is the reason why I insist that my patients cannot get well unless they learn to control their temperamental cycles." (MHTWT, p. 398)

SETBACK

"Patients come to me and tell me, 'Well, I did very well for so-and-so many months, but today I have symptoms again.' And I ask myself, is that so exceptional, that a man who has done well gets symptoms again? Has he never heard of the setback that is very common and average with people who suffer?" (MFMA, p. 20)

"A setback disappears in minutes-perhaps in half an hour, but usually in minutes, frequently in seconds-if you expect it and don't let it alarm you...What makes the setback... so formidable is that it alarms you. That's all." (MFMA, p. 241)

"Our method is built on the principle that in minor complications like nervous symptoms-even if they are severe they are only minor complications-in minor complications you must set your will against fate, and once you set your will against fate, you relax, and nature has then an opportunity to correct the complication because our body, this means nature, is a self-repairing machine." (MFMA, p 17)

"If life has no frustration, if life were all happiness and carefree living, then it would be boring. You would be surfeited with a life [of] all smoothness, all proceeding on the same level, no downs, no dips, no frustrations, no disappointments. That is boredom. Expect frustrations all over, all the time. And if you expect them, then you will not be disappointed. Then you will be frustrated, and that will be no disappointment because you expected it." (MFMA, p. 86-87)

"We in Recovery have pondered this problem, and we have asked ourselves, 'Why does the patient get the setback?' and we could not find the answer. We could only find the answer to the question whether the setback can be kept mild or must be degenerating to a severe condition. And you know I have told you, if you expect the setback, if you are sure or convinced that the setback will come, but you can handle it by not being alarmed about it, then the setback will be mild. Otherwise, it will be severe." (MFMA, p. 90)

"The patient hates to tell that he has improved, and the reason you will perhaps now see. That patient, after the first setback, becomes afraid of improving. Once the setback sets in again, the patient knows by now that he or she can do what they ought to do. But they have frightful palpitations and head pressures, so they lie down and don't do anything. But now they have no longer a consolation that fate is against them because they had experienced an improvement...And now the patient can no longer have the conviction that that is unavoidable, that the patient cannot do what he or she ought to do." (MFMA, p. 91)

SIMPLICITY

"Don't expect that your condition, being as complex as it is-and I don't deny that-requires complex methods to check it and to conquer it. That's not so. The simple method is always the superior procedure." (MFMA, p. 76)

"Recovery refuses to be modern, and the leadership which it supplies aims precisely at teaching you how to conquer confused ideas and perturbed emotions through simplicity of thinking and humility of feeling." (MHTWT, p. 140)

"Recovery stands for simplicity. Its systems of instruction and training are meant to enable the plain, humble and untutored patient to practice self-help. An objective of this kind cannot be achieved by means of involved explanations and complex techniques. Self-help in psychiatric after-care calls for simple methods of interpreting and manipulating symptoms. It is for this reason that Recovery offers to its members plain common sense instead of intricate philosophies and artless techniques of training in place of elaborate procedures." (MHTWT, p. 325)

"The training process in Recovery…consists in a simple phrase, in making the patient realize that he is in apprenticeship." (MFMA, p. 60)

SLEEP

"With physically healthy persons, sleep never fails to remove fatigue…to sleep means to rest the muscles. How can your muscles be fatigued if they are rested?" (MHTWT, p. 339)

Dr. Low's response to a patient who claimed he didn't sleep at all: "I must challenge your statement that you couldn't sleep although you stayed in bed for hours. That may happen occasionally and does happen with great regularity in the instance of persons suffering from acute distressing ailments. Otherwise, *to lie in bed for hours means to sleep part of the hours.* The sleep may be of poor quality and may proceed in fitful snatches. After each snatch you awaken having the feeling that you 'did not sleep a wink.' Nevertheless, you slept a considerable portion of the time which you spent in bed." (MHTWT, p. 350-351)

"Fear can be remedied only by the certain knowledge that no danger threatens. You cannot gain this knowledge from your own experience which is amateurish and limited to the acquaintance with one single case. What must guide you is my authoritative knowledge which is based on solid study and expert observation. This alone can give you the conviction that no danger whatever attends a night spent in bed even if you feel you 'haven't slept a wink.' " (MHTWT, p. 357)

SPONTANEITY

"If anybody can tell himself, 'I just go ahead and do things and nothing interferes with my actions. I start to act out my intention, and there, without hesitation, without friction, without fear, I accomplish it.' That's what we call *self-management*. But if the doctor has to step in-or the mother and father, or the neighbor or a friend-and urge you to do something against your inclination, then you are subjected to foreign management. And you don't act in the spirit of self-management. Then you lose your pride, your self-respect, your self-confidence, and you are filled with self-consciousness, self-distrust. You don't feel that you can depend on your own inner structures." (MFMA, p. 239-240)

"Spontaneity is interfered with or destroyed by self-consciousness... self-consciousness is produced by the fact that two contradictory intentions endeavor to make the muscles express two different ideas at the same time. The muscles are thrown into disorder expressing portions of the one idea and fragments of the other with the result that the speech loses clarity and gives the impression of confusion." (MHTWT, p. 413-414)

"The patients are taken care of here in Recovery, and you know we have developed techniques which, without great trouble, make the patient[s] resume their self-management. Our techniques make the patients, if they come here regularly, make the patients relax. And with relaxation, there is no fear, and without fear, self-management is restored, and with it, that precious thing that we call *spontaneity of action*." (MFMA, p. 240)

SPOTTING

"If you have the modesty and humility to know that you don't know, your spotting will be of the most perfect and exquisite quality." (Selections, p. 66)

"Your self-appointed expectations are intuitive productions of your brain...Being pushed back into the background of your consciousness, they are not known to you. You will also understand that the method of getting rid of your harmful and health-wrecking expectations is the proper use of our spotting techniques. What must be spotted is the intuitive meaning of your self-appointments. If your spotting is done correctly, after due Recovery training, you will be able to use your conscious Will for the purpose of saying a resounding "No" to your intuitive strivings and to stop them effectively through control of muscles." (Selections, p. 38)

"The art of spotting is inborn, apart from instruction and training, but is put into practice only when the proper incentive is operating... everybody is ready and frequently itching to spot the erroneous thought and faulty action of other persons. The incentive is here to display superior intelligence by exposing others as lacking it. There is no such incentive to expose, that is, to spot one's own inadequacies of thought and action. Expressing it otherwise: Foreign spotting is pleasure and is engaged in with gusto. Self-spotting is or may be painful and is graciously dispensed with." (Selections, p. 42)

"A few remarks...about 'spotting.' You know the phrase 'to spot somebody in a crowd.' Ordinarily, a single man is lost in a crowd. He is hidden from sight, obscured by the multitude. Once you have sighted him he is spotted. His identity is now clearly discerned and sorted out from the mass. In other words, spotting means to bring into plain sight what has been invisible or obscured." (Selections, p. 81-82)

"There are so many things I do not understand that it would be physically impossible to catalogue them. I do not understand why, on some morning I arise and find myself devoid of my customary energy, or why on some occasions I am sprightly and mentally alert and on other occasions my spirit seems to have gone from me and my disposition reaches a low ebb of dullness and indolence that is truly appalling. And I do not understand at all why if I have some unfathomable difficulty it lasts five minutes the one day and two or three hours the other. All of this is beyond my comprehension. Fortunately, it is immaterial whether a nervous condition is or is not understood. What counts is the knowledge that every nervous symptom, no matter how mysterious and incomprehensible, can be controlled through spotting thoughts and commanding muscles. You see, no matter what subject you patients will bring up, my answer is invariably and monotonously: Spot your thoughts and command your muscles!" (Selections, p. 115-116)

"Tempers and dispositions can be changed provided the one displaying them (1) acquires *insight* and realizes the need for a change of manners, (2) is inspired with the determination to effect the necessary change." (P v. P, p. 84)

"After you finish dressing or eating you do not protest that you had a right to dress or eat. Under ordinary circumstances the propriety and justification of the act is not contested by any person or standard. You are not called upon to offer apologies or excuses for innocent behavior of this kind. Should, however, a person after consuming a meal, exclaim, 'Don't you think I had a right to eat?' you would instantly know that the eater himself thought the propriety of his act might be challenged and had to be justified. Mark it: whenever a person insists on being right he either was or felt he was challenged." (P v. P, p. 90)

"Spotting means for you to be perpetually on guard against your inveterate tendency to 'do your own thinking' when observing a symptom and its accompanying temperamental reaction. It means a ruthless determination to eliminate self-diagnosing and thus to do away with panics, vicious cycles and endless horrors of agony." (MHTWT, p. 227)

"If my patients are to be rid of their symptoms they must learn to dispense with the vanities of claiming superior knowledge and to cultivate the humility of realizing their limited efficiency in thinking and acting. This requires continuous and unrelenting spotting, the pre-eminent method of self-control taught you in Recovery." (MHTWT, p. 164)

"Will you understand that spotting means primarily to avoid extremes, to avoid extremes above and below…It's a great satisfaction to be satisfied. One doesn't have to be happy. To be in good spirits, why must they be high spirits? And it's not so bad to be dissatisfied. But the patient being dissatisfied immediately says, 'I am the unhappiest person, the unluckiest person, why must everything happen to me?' Haven't you heard that? 'Everything,' the patient speaks in terms of 'everything,' which is nonsense. There are minutes at least when he feels good. But he has the idea things are either always or never. Do you understand these are all extremes?" (MFMA, p. 433)

"Spotting does not mean what you say, not even what you think consciously. All of this is in the foreground of consciousness. And the foreground of consciousness does not have to be spotted. That is revealed to you either in your conscious thoughts or in your conscious statements. And anything that is conscious with you, you don't have to spot. You know it. But that's all you know, and that's very little." (MFMA, p. 163)

"The Recovery teaching is not merely to control temper but to do what is needed in order to control temper. And what is needed for the control of temper is spotting." (MFMA, p. 161)

"If a youngster tells an experienced, elderly person the truth, then that youngster obviously thinks he knows the truth. And that's an awfully difficult task, to know the truth. There are many truths that I struggle with, and I am no longer a youngster, I will assure you. And I still struggle with endless truths and I don't find them. It's an extremely difficult task to know what is the truth and what is not." (MFMA, p. 162-163)

"If you want to get from the outer expression of a person, or of yourself, to the inner experience of that person, or yourself, you can't just listen to what a person says or what you yourself say. You must travel from the outer expression to the inner experience, and that's what we call *spotting*." (MFMA, p. 163)

"If somebody asks me, 'Will we go here or there; will we do this or that?' and I say, 'We'll see,' that has a multiplicity of meanings. But one meaning is outstanding among this variety of meanings, and it signifies that I have the power to decide. 'We'll see.' This means, 'I will not give you an answer. You better wait.'" (MFMA, p.201-202)

"I have for years scoured the textbooks, the encyclopedias to find some lead towards finding the meanings underneath sentences and underneath reactions. And I may tell you I have found very little in the literature about this subject. But that thing that I call here *finding the meaning underneath statements and underneath actions,* that's precisely what we mean by *spotting.*" (MFMA, p. 202-203)

"Whatever is conscious is at the surface of thinking. And anybody can understand and, at the same time, explain the surface appearances of the mind, but the surface only. Everything else requires laborious training. If you want to go down to the depths of meanings, both with regard to statements or reactions, you have to make a special study. The study will require you to learn the techniques of spotting." (MFMA, p. 204)

"Do you understand now what we mean by spotting? Spotting means not to look at the surface of the thing. That needs no spotting because it needs no explanation. Everybody understands that and can express it discursively. Nor does spotting mean to get at the depths through intuition. That's very good. It's good to have some intuition. But that will not tell you exactly and clearly why you got angry, why you developed temper, why you felt frustrated. You will only feel it, but you will not be able to know it clearly and to explain it lucidly. Spotting means to look underneath statements and reactions and then know consciously what they mean, not intuitively-consciously, or, as I called it before, *discursively.* And you see, since we have introduced this matter of spotting, our patients have gradually learned or are learning gradually to look into their depths and perhaps into the depths of people around them like husbands, friends, and so forth. But I think this is of no great importance. What is important is that patients are now able to look into themselves and not merely to feel and sense intuitively what is at the base of their reaction but to know it consciously and discursively." (MFMA, p. 205-206)

"Spotting is so intricate, so complex that it requires continuous training. Continuous. I mean it. And I tell you how continuous it must be and must be done. I have stumbled on this subject of spotting about fifteen years ago. And in the meantime, I have made it a life task to study this subject. And I tell you I have studied it very perseveringly, day after day, I must say hour after hour, in all these fifteen years. And you should think that now I am a master of spotting. But I am not yet. And whether I will ever be, I don't know. I'm still too slow in finding meanings underneath statements and reactions, far too slow to suit me, although you may be certain that I am much faster than anyone is who has not studied and learned the technique." (MFMA, p. 207)

"If you want to gain good control and good ability of spotting, then you must turn spotting into a habit, and you can't acquire a habit in two days, not in two weeks. If you acquire it in two years, then you are very lucky." (MFMA, p. 232)

"Spotting, among other things, means look into yourself, watch your statements, your thoughts, your wishes, and don't interpret them in such a manner that they do you harm." (MFMA, p. 258)

"A dog jumps at you, and you get scared...you formed the belief that there is danger. Then you looked at the dog, and you formed the belief there is no danger. The first belief, that there was danger, made you tense. The second belief, there is no danger, removed the tenseness. It wasn't done by the dog. The dog couldn't have removed the tenseness. The dog removed himself, but not the tenseness. And this simple example will show you what we mean by spotting." (MFMA, p. 266)

STIGMA

"You are not responsible, first, for the fact that you have weak nerves. Second, you are not responsible for the fact that somebody else gets well more quickly than you do. Nobody will be fair if he holds that against you, because there are so-called individual differences...for which fate is responsible and not you and your will." (MFMA, p. 14)

"Anyone of you who has developed a nervous ailment has suffered a happening that happened to you. You didn't manufacture it through your character." (MFMA, p. 121)

"The patient...feels ashamed of the fact that his nervous system is weak. This is...vanity. That patient is vain enough to expect that all his systems must be perfect. I have yet to see a human being that has nothing but perfect systems." (MFMA, p. 33)

"Don't listen to anybody who will tell you [that] once you have had a severe nervous or mental condition that you will never come back. That's, of course, arrant nonsense, and don't listen to such prophets of doom." (MFMA, p. 69)

"Let me tell you that this excuse that 'I have had weak nerves all my life' does not count a thing in point of curability. Every nervous condition can be cured, regardless of its duration-by the way, also regardless of its intensity." (MFMA, p. 367)

"The very leaders of humanity have had outrageously distressing nervous troubles. You will admit that Abraham Lincoln was a leader of humanity, but he suffered precisely from the manic-depressive conditions from which my patients are suffering. And the great Washington was not a very relaxed person. He had all kinds of complaints that we now call *nervous*. And if you go further than those and roam through the literature of every nation, to the art record of every nation, the higher you rise in the scale of human personalities, the more do you encounter people, great men, geniuses, that are racked by nervous symptoms, and some of them by mental symptoms. Some of them, naturally, have landed in state institutions, quite a number of them." (MFMA, p. 75-76)

"Now let me tell you, when you develop a poor resistance in your nervous system, whether you develop it or whether it is born with you does not matter, but if you have a poor resistance, that was done by fate. You simply don't know yourself, how to arrange it that you create a poor resistance...You did not want to have poor resistance, by no means. And so all of you, when you had your first symptoms, or your first break, or your first decline in nervous reactions, you had it as a heritage from fate. You were not responsible for what happened to you." (MFMA, p. 12-13)

"Some of you have had a mental sickness, but now you are out of it, and your nervous system is either strengthened-perhaps quite strong-or if it is still weak, what of it? A weakness of the nervous system can certainly be taken care of here." (MFMA, p. 33)

"Nobody would draw the conclusion that somebody whom one sees distressed suffers from a nervous symptom, from a panic, from a vicious cycle. Hardly anybody will ever do that with a stranger. One only sees that he is somehow upset, and one interprets this upset as stemming from an average cause, this means business difficulties, family difficulties, or any other kind of such average difficulty. But the patient always thinks-or is inclined always to think-that his cheeks show the tenseness to such an extent that everybody notices it. And everybody then knows that he is a nervous or a former mental patient, which is, of course, stark nonsense. You people here credit the average person with an extreme degree of penetration of insight. He hasn't got it, and I don't have it either." (MFMA, p. 250)

"A patient, even after the patient has improved to a great extent, nevertheless has not necessarily acquired the art of exposing himself or herself to the public eye. That's a difficult thing not only for patients. But patients have gone through a long extended period in which they have been hiding themselves, not literally, but they have been hiding themselves in the sense of making a secret of their suffering, of which they were ashamed. Perhaps not every patient has done that. But there are very few who did not hide their suffering, their symptoms, and, as they thought of it, their disgrace. And that's what we call *the stigma of nervous and mental ailments*." (MFMA, p. 249)

SUFFERING

"Suffering can either be reported objectively or complained about subjectively...Stop the muscular habit of complaining, and you will put an end to the mental habit of defeatism." (Selections, p. 45)

"Patients come to me and tell me, 'Well, I did very well for so-and-so many months, but today I have symptoms again.' And I ask myself, is that so exceptional, that a man who has done well gets symptoms again? Has he never heard of the setback that is very common and average with people who suffer?" (MFMA, p. 20)

"The poor wretch that falls into my hands is unlucky because from me he can't expect instant relief. I will tell him to wait. You know that. He has to show patience, and the very least thing that the patient wants to show is patience. He wants instant relief or as speedy relief as possible because his suffering is really outrageous… Of course, I don't have to tell you that I give you instant relief very frequently, too. But I pooh-pooh the value of instant relief. That will never cure you." (MFMA, p. 272)

"Why do you want relief? The reason is that suffering is something that naturally is most unpleasant. It's painful. It's agonizing. Suffering is the reverse of being comfortable. But let me tell you that every individual in this world craves to have a comfortable life." (MFMA, p. 273)

"Health cannot be secured in five seconds, but the patient wants relief in five seconds and preferably in half a second. Oh, it sounds laughable, I agree with you. And yet the patient can get some relief in a second or two. He can, for instance, at that moment, get attention, and sympathy, and affection. And he can be given the opportunity to talk about his suffering. That gives him some relief. All of this. The attention that is given him supplies a modicum, almost a minimum, of relief. But it's gone in a second." (MFMA, p. 285)

SUGGESTIBILITY

"There is too much talk about collapses and the danger of heart diseases and the danger of cancer. Cancer is dangerous. I don't deny that. Heart diseases are dangerous. But if you constantly talk and think and hear about the danger of organic diseases, you will not develop an organic disease from this. That will not cause any damage in you. It will, however, cause fear, and the fear will cause a psychological disorder." (MFMA, p. 461)

SYMPTOMS

" [My patients] shy away, persistently and doggedly, from the total view that their symptoms are of the average variety although more persistent in duration and more resistant to management." (MHTWT, p. 212-213)

"Both temper and symptom run their course, and you cannot stop them by an effort of the will as you can do with thoughts and muscular action." (MHTWT, p. 388)

"The fundamental principle of Recovery [is] that symptoms can be conquered by means of simple and innocent procedures initiated by the patient, i.e., through self-help." (MHTWT, p. 126)

"If I ask my patients to be realistic instead of sentimental, if I insist that they renounce their romantic sense of exceptionality in favor of sober self-accounting in terms of averageness, I refer to the attitude they are supposed to take with regard to their symptoms. There they must not indulge in sentimental dreams of exceptionality; there they must plant themselves solidly on the ground of realistic averageness." (MHTWT, p. 84-85)

"Once you have accomplished a conquest over a nervous symptom, your victory is astounding. Ordinarily people don't do that." (MFMA, p. 33)

"With reference to his symptoms a nervous patient must be genuine in feeling and sincere in thought." (MHTWT, p. 189)

"Nervousness and nervous symptoms are universal and average and...to get well means to become again an average nervous person who experiences nervous reactions in many phases of his life but has implicit confidence in the trustworthiness of his basic functions." (Selections, p. 10)

"The patient does not want to be convinced that his symptoms are harmless. His convictions tend the opposite way. What he wants to see and believe is the emergency nature of his condition, not its harmlessness. The element of emergency he spotlights, the element of harmlessness he blindspots." (Selections, p. 127)

"Mark it: whenever you do not know whether you are right or wrong you are bound to be tense." (P v. P, p. 75)

"My supreme and only duty is to relieve my patients of their agonies. And if their panics and vicious cycles result from their faulty use of the thinking process I shall advise them to throw overboard the rubbish of modern slogans and let me do their thinking in the matter of interpreting and concluding with regard to symptoms." (MHTWT, p. 226)

"Organic disturbances, that is, complications created by Fate, act indiscriminately and without selection. They may strike any person at any time in any place. Once they have struck they do not pick out shrewdly certain occasions in which they will make a stage appearance or certain others in which they will keep cunningly off the stage. If a symptom is regularly present in one set of conditions and regularly absent in another, the judicious choice cannot be the result of Fate which is never selective. It must be the outflow of Will whose very function is to choose and select." (Selections, p. 60)

"You can throw off any nervous symptom at any time for a few seconds or minutes if you spot them as distressing but not dangerous. The symptom will come back in the next minute or so. But you can get rid of it again for a short while, and then again and again and before long you will be rid of the trouble for hours or for days. The symptom will return and keep returning but in the end you will bring it under control by plugging away at it." (MHTWT, p. 139)

"Nervous symptoms are the result of tenseness and if you 'spot them as distressing but not dangerous' you dismiss the idea of danger; and without the thought of danger in your brain you feel safe; and if you feel safe you relax; and if you relax you lose your tenseness; and with tenseness gone the symptom disappears. What can be more simple, what more easy to believe and more thoroughly in accord with sense?" (MHTWT, p. 140)

"My supreme and only duty is to relieve my patients of their agonies. And if their panics and vicious cycles result from their faulty use of the thinking process I shall advise them to throw overboard the rubbish of modern slogans and let me do their thinking in the matter of interpreting and concluding with regard to symptoms." (MHTWT, p. 226)

"Spotting means for you to be perpetually on guard against your inveterate tendency to 'do your own thinking' when observing a symptom and its accompanying temperamental reaction. It means a ruthless determination to eliminate self-diagnosing and thus to do away with panics, vicious cycles and endless horrors of agony." (MHTWT, p. 227)

"If my patients are to be rid of their symptoms they must learn to dispense with the vanities of claiming superior knowledge and to cultivate the humility of realizing their limited efficiency in thinking and acting. This requires continuous and unrelenting spotting, the pre-eminent method of self-control taught you in Recovery." (MHTWT, p. 164)

"With a relaxed brain, there can be no nervous symptom. But the relaxation must be a real relaxation. It must be thorough, not just something that you call, 'Oh, I feel better.' That's no relaxation. It must be a real relaxation. And in order to learn how to relax thoroughly, that takes time." (MFMA, p. 381)

"When you have palpitations, it's very easy and no effort whatever to run to the phone and call the doctor. That's easy. That's comfort, or the prospect of comfort. Here in this organization you are trained to stand discomfort and to make a strenuous effort. And a supreme effort for a nervous patient is to stand his symptoms, not to run to the phone to call the physician, and it's remarkable what you do when you decide to stand the discomfort of the symptom." (MFMA, p. 5)

"Accept my diagnosis. I have the experience, of course, with thousands of conditions and patients. You have the experience with your own case. That's no experience. That is the experience of one case. And even if you say that you have a very close and intimate knowledge of your case, I grant you, you have. You have the knowledge that I don't have. I don't know whether your heart is now palpitating, whether your stomach is tightening up right now. I don't know that. You know, but do you understand what that means? Do you understand whether that means danger or security? You feel what you feel inside, but you don't know what it means. It is only the diagnosis, made by a competent and experienced man, that gives the meaning to your suffering, and that's, of course, very important. If I [know] what your condition signifies, then I can pick the correct treatment according to my experience, which is seasoned." (MFMA, p 132)

"Any one of you who has conquered one set of symptoms, or more symptoms and some sets of symptoms, has accomplished something that is by no means common. Indeed, it's very rare, except here in Recovery, where it is not rare…Ordinarily if people have nervous symptoms, these nervous symptoms set up vicious cycles, and in time they grow worse and worse, not better. And mark it: you have accomplished your victory over your nervous troubles, not by tricks, not by somebody pulling a trick on you, or you pulling a trick on yourself, but by exercising your will power by means of a method that I have taught you. You owe the conquest over the symptom to your own strength, not to my strength, not to my tricks or stratagems. And why you should not finally get to the point where you acquire pride because of what you have accomplished in your handling of your symptoms-well, I don't know why you don't acquire this pride." (MFMA, p. 33-34)

"If somebody tells a patient, 'Oh, you imagine your headaches,' what does he mean by that? He means you manufacture them.

He means you haven't had, or you don't have, a headache. You merely imagine it. You merely believe you have one. That's a very ribald [worthless] statement. Who is competent to say that he feels a headache except the one who has it? I, the physician, don't know whether he right now has a headache or not. But if the patient tells me he has a headache, why should I doubt that? The patient doesn't come to me for fun. He comes in a serious endeavor, and, in addition, he even pays a fee, and why he should pay a fee for a fib that he tells me, I don't know. So will you please, will you please drop this silly suspicion that nervous patients imagine their headaches." (MFMA, p. 133-134)

"You want to be superior. This means you depend on others to either recognize you, to give you credit as being not just average, to give you the honor of constantly catering to you, perhaps do you the favor of constantly flattering you. And if you don't get credit and if you don't get honor and if you don't get flattery, then you become tense because you expect it and you don't get it. And therefore vanity and the striving for perfection is harmful, particularly to the nervous patient. Because since vanity is usually not accomplished, since being vain you don't get people to give you the due credit and flattery and honor, therefore you become tense. Vanity always makes you tense. And if you are a nervous patient, and your vanity makes you tense, the tenseness creates symptoms, and you can't get well. At least you can't get well quickly, in due time." (MFMA, p. 155)

"A nervous ailment is recognized by its symptoms, and these symptoms are …due to tenseness and, as far as I know, to nothing else if an organic ailment has been ruled out." (MFMA, p. 222)

"A symptom is a new habit that the patient has developed through tenseness." (MFMA, p. 235)

"All the experiences of a nervous patient can be reduced to the fact that he develops tenseness. Without tenseness, the patient would relax, normally relax. He would have average relaxation. But with tenseness, relaxation is gone. And if relaxation is gone and tenseness installs itself on an enduring basis, then symptoms appear." (MFMA, p. 265)

"Nature bungles physical diseases that have developed to some extent, but nature is the highest authority for curing simple disturbances. And if I diagnose you as a nervous patient, then be certain that all your symptoms are simple disturbances and nothing else. No sickness. And simple disturbances can be corrected by the body." (MFMA, p. 4)

TEMPER

"Temper is the outcome of an inner arrogance which sets itself up as judge of who is right and who is wrong. This arrogance is due to the sense of one's own importance and cannot be overcome unless the sense of humor is cultivated to the point where humility, plainness and averageness take the place of arrogance, exceptionality and self-importance." (MHTWT, p. 109-110)

"Both temper and symptom run their course, and you cannot stop them by an effort of the will as you can do with thoughts and muscular action." (MHTWT, p. 388)

"What patients are taught in Recovery is to curb their tempers and to leave the original responses to run their course." (MHTWT, p. 169)

"The wildest temper outburst can be checked instantly if you take the objective attitude that you are not the judge as to who is right or wrong." (MHTWT, p. 127)

"If you have had any reaction that you might be ashamed of, be certain I had it and all humanity had it, except the saints." (MFMA, p. 43)

"Whether you are right or wrong is immaterial. Temper is a matter of breeding, not of right and wrong." (Lost and Found, Vol. 2, No. 4, 1939 reprinted in Recovery Reporter, Vol. 63, No. 2, March-April 2000)

"Nobody loses his temper unless he is or feels he is wronged or insulted intentionally." (MHTWT, p. 392)

"In my more than thirty years of intensive experience with patients I have met nothing but average cases. In all of them I have observed the following pattern: There are the average run of symptoms which are due to average type of tenseness, and the tenseness is created or maintained by either temper or self-diagnosing or by both. And the average patient can easily discover within himself both temper and self-diagnosing." (Selections, p. 109)

"It is a popular belief contrary to actual experience that the spirit of service is generously displayed in the home sphere and that the spirit of domination increases the more the sphere of action includes strangers...the average individual tries his best to be friendly and courteous with the stranger but loses his temper frequently with those familiar to him and is likely to be rude and impatient with his intimates. The reason for this discriminating behavior is clear; you risk nothing or little if you are harsh and brusque with your son, father, or mother. They are helpless in the face of your rudeness. What disciplinary measure can a mother resort to if her son is intractable? She cannot very well eject him and deny him his share of family life...Let the same son display his rudeness in the presence of strangers, and he will not be permitted to victimize any of them. They will not hesitate to pay him back in kind." (P v. P, p. 48-49)

"This assurance of oneself being right and the other person wrong is the essential basis of what I described as the domestic attitude of the problem adult. It is the rock on which most unsuccessful marital relations are currently wrecked." (P v. P, p. 52)

"It may be stated as a fact that if a person is possessed of a domineering temper he will *conceal* it in words and acts but *reveal* it in tone, gesture and feature." (P v. P, p. 52)

"I grant that it would be difficult to change a person's nature. But a man's temper is by no means his nature. At any rate, the average man's temper is not necessarily derived from natural inheritance. It is a far safer assumption that it is acquired through a process of mis-education." (P v. P, p. 60-61)

"Few persons dare give way to their 'nature' if it runs counter to public opinion...In days bygone, public opinion tolerated wife beating and cruelty to children and animals. The result was that husbands, fathers and drivers who were so disposed yielded to their 'nature' and indulged in orgies of cruelty. Today, when public opinion has definitely determined that cruelty to defenseless creatures is uncalled-for by the circumstances of civilized life, husbands, fathers and drivers seem to have discovered that their 'nature' contains an unexpected strain of kindness." (P v. P, p. 61)

"I think it is about time to create within our group the type of public opinion that will set its face solidly against bullying and domineering no matter how skillful its disguise. It seems to me we should not hesitate to cultivate in our midst an attitude that will condemn all varieties of domestic cruelty with uncompromising severity. Then we will be the first group of numerical importance that will do away with that lethal blight of human relations: the dual conditional standard which prohibits rudeness outside the family circle and sanctions or at least tolerates it inside the home. We, the members of the Recovery, Inc. group, have pioneered in so many ways. Why not pioneer in matters of domestic adjustment? Why should we not try to create our own brand of public opinion?" (P v. P, p. 64)

"The public at large considers temper the legitimate offspring of 'human nature' and thus declares it as unalterable and inaccessible to education as 'nature itself.' Recovery, Inc. rejects with vigor the claim to unalterability and brands uncontrolled temper as the illegitimate offspring of a public opinion oblivious to its duties and responsibilities...To Recovery, Inc. heredity is no brief for an unrestrained laissez-faire attitude, and 'nature' no carte blanche for domestic cruelty. Both patients and relatives are made to realize that the 'nature' which they inherited is subject to the influence of training and self-discipline. In emphasizing the necessity for self-discipline the author does not intend to assume the function of a moralist or uplift crusader but to perform the plain duty of the

physician whose pursuit is to cure effects by removing their causes."
(P v. P, p. 71-72)

"Forever afraid of being wrong, a conflict-torn or dilemma-plagued individual is anxious to convince himself that, in actual fact, he is right...The most effective method of establishing one's claim to being right is a stubborn insistence on being listened to, on getting one's suggestions accepted and one's dictates acted on. This secures a sense of mastery and disposes, for the moment, of the suspicion of one's being `wrong. Persons embroiled in perpetual inner conflicts are, therefore, eager to gain mastery over the partner. The common tendency to be domineering has here its root. It begins with the sense of being wrong, proceeds to the claim to be right, and ends in the overwhelming desire to dominate each and every situation." (P v. P, p. 78)

"Everybody suffers from deep-seated conflicts. But it is not true that everybody has poor manners. In other words, the presence of conflicts is no valid excuse for bad behavior and poor adjustment. Conflicts *explain* temper but do not *excuse* it." (P v. P, p. 81)

"Gossip is a mechanism capable of relieving the tenseness caused by conflicts. It gives relief by convincing you that the 'other fellow' is wrong, so atrociously wrong that your failing in this respect must appear very small, indeed. Bullying, sarcasm, ridicule are other such mechanisms. They all tend to demonstrate the wrongness, weakness, helplessness, and inadequacy of others. After bullying, ridiculing, or reprimanding others you have the doubtful distinction of having scored a victory. It is this sense of being victorious that gives you the pleasure of which I spoke when I stated that poor manners are cultivated and permitted to become set habits 'because a premium of secret pleasure is placed on them'." (P v. P, p. 82-83)

"Tempers and dispositions can be changed provided the one displaying them (1) acquires *insight* and realizes the need for a change of manners, (2) is inspired with the determination to effect the necessary change." (P v. P, p. 84)

"If a man secures from an act the pleasurable feeling of being right he will refuse to abandon it and *choose* to continue. But for the premium of pleasure that rests on temperamental behavior a change of temper would be as easy as a change in clothing. The obvious inference is that in order to make men control their tempers they must be made to realize that the claim to be right is no justification for the will to be rude." (P v. P, p. 90)

"This is the crux of domestic discord in practically all its manifestations: one partner bullies the other and has the unobscured insight that bullying is indefensible. But the insight is without effect because it is swept aside by the self-deception that the bullying is done "by right." Do you see the involved tragedy? Humans are so constituted that they relish a "fight for rights." If they manage to convince themselves that their fight is one for "rights" the prospects are they will be reluctant to cease fighting and will *choose* to continue. The result will be the 'temperamental deadlock'." (P v. P, p. 92)

"There are occasions-rare in civilized groups-when men fight for *objective realities*. There are occasions when they are *really and objectively* assaulted and insulted. There are other occasions when vicious, scheming, unscrupulous persons attempt to gain an unfair advantage over them. Occasions of this kind call for fight. But that fight is, as a rule, fought coolly, deliberately, with slow moves and well-calculated measures. The impulsive outburst, the rise of temper, and sudden attack are, as a rule foreign to such realistic struggles...I wish you would grasp this fundamental distinction: fights for realities are rare in the daily round of average life, and the fights encountered in domestic discord are almost invariably centered around the imaginary issue of 'being right'." (P v. P, p. 93)

"At the risk of being intolerably monotonous and repetitious I shall recite the well-known fact that temperamental persons, as a rule, display their tempers solely or mainly with the members of their immediate family and with their employees. In the company of strangers and friends, and particularly in the presence of 'important' people, like superiors, hosts and hostesses, their nature is pleasingly tamed, their instinct neatly controlled and their heredity conveniently forgotten. Most of it is clearly not inborn but acquired." (P v. P, p. 100)

"Temperamental persons fight for infantile symbols rather than adult realities." (P v. P, p. 112)

"The salesgirl who is a paragon of sweetness and geniality when provoked by overbearing customers may be impatient, irritable and explosive with members of her own family...Obviously, some incentive is operating in the sales room which induces the girl to exercise control, while at home this incentive is missing. You will have no difficulty realizing that the incentive I am speaking of is the determination to keep the job. We conclude that temper can be effectively curbed by a powerful determining *incentive*. We draw the further inference that domestic discord could be disposed of if powerful incentives for temper control could be established at home." (P v. P, p. 125)

"At the end of a temper tantrum there is always the feeling of pleasure and, at its beginning, the anticipation of pleasure. This is the crux of the issue of temper: the anticipation of pleasure places a premium on the outburst. To curb temper, then, means to forego a keen pleasure. And the average person is not easily induced to give up pleasure even if it is a pleasure that hurts. Do you realize now why temper control is so difficult to achieve?" (P v. P, p. 129-130)

"In temper outbursts the irrational impulse is temporarily halted by rational insight but finally sanctioned by rationalizing self-deception." (P v. P, p. 131)

"It is the process of rationalization that is most apt to cloud insight and block its operation...Rationalization makes 'right' what insight declares 'wrong' and endorses as socially desirable what insight condemns as socially reprehensible." (P v. P, p. 132)

"Whether you check or release your temper depends on how you expect others to behave…men with explosive tempers expect too much consideration from their fellows and view their motives and intentions with too much suspicion." (P v. P, p. 138)

"Knowing the obstinacy and conservatism of 'human nature', I do not for a moment think of asking you to eliminate your temperamental disposition. All I ask you is not to nurse, tend and cultivate it until it hardens into an inveterate predisposition. This you can do by withholding approval and endorsement during the stage of the temperamental after-effect. If you do that, the recovered patient, after leaving the hospital, will return to a home which, while not free from temperamental outbursts, will not be continually rocked by fierce eruptions and violent explosions." (P v. P, p. 161)

"In temper a right is subjectively claimed and force objectively used." (MHTWT, p. 48)

"Opinions interpret facts. It ought to be clear to you by now that both the opinions and interpretations are guesses, hence, imaginations. It ought to be just as clear that facts are realities. Temper contains one opinion and many facts. The opinion is that of right and wrong. The facts are the sensations, feelings, impulses and acts (verbal and muscular) which are experienced or expressed in the temperamental sequence." (MHTWT, p. 49)

"My patients claim they suffer from frightening sensations, overpowering impulses, torturing thoughts and devitalized feelings. But I tell them that this is a half-truth at best; that what they actually suffer from is—their philosophy. And if their philosophy is based on the assumption that in their spells and tantrums their feelings are real and their thoughts are right, well, that is precisely the philosophy of temper. In the ordinary burst of temper, whether it be presymptomatic or postsymptomatic, you *feel* the insult or injury was a 'real' outrage, and *think* you are 'right' in considering it a deliberate hurt." (MHTWT, p. 75)

"It is the distinctive mark of the so-called intellectual to emphasize or over-emphasize one side of an issue only, usually his own side, and to look away from the other side. Much of what I have told you in the past ten years about temper can be safely condensed in the one concise formulation: temper is, among other things, the result of an intellectual blindness to the 'other side of the story'. " (MHTWT, p. 158-159)

"Feelings should be expressed. This does not mean they ought to be acted on or acted out. It merely means they should be communicated to or shared with somebody who can be trusted to understand them…They lend themselves to matter-of-fact discussion and calm appraisal. But temper, involving a claim to being right, cannot be reported objectively, calmly and matter-of-factly. It invariably leads to arguments, debates and rebuttals." (MHTWT, p. 177-178)

"If a father loves his children and constantly teases them so that they really become distracted, or he constantly says *no* when they ask for something, don't tell me that is love. That father may still love the children, but his love is outstripped by something that we call *domination*. He has no respect for the desires of the children. The children have no desire to constantly [be] teased. They have certainly no desire to be constantly treated with *no*, with negativism." (MFMA, p. 80)

"I am not at all concerned with your being natural and human. My sole objective is to rid you of your symptoms. You seem to think it is your natural and human privilege to exercise your temper. It is just as natural and human to eat steak. But if a man is suffering from a gastric upset he'd better relinquish his 'natural and human right' to steak dinners. Are you willing to give up your temper for the sake of your health?" (MHTWT, p. 387)

"The common variety of temper is a condition in which one person draws the intuitive conclusion that another person intends to offend him…in order to gain control over his temper a person must learn through continuous practice to avoid the intuitive conclusion of a deliberate insult which precedes the temperamental outburst." (MHTWT, p. 395)

"It takes real courage to stop temper short, much more than to give way to it. That's easy. A dog can do that." (MDO, p. 228)

"The Recovery teaching is not merely to control temper but to do what is needed in order to control temper. And what is needed for the control of temper is spotting." (MFMA, p. 161)

"If you want to get rid of your nervous symptoms, you must establish, or re-establish, relaxation. You can call it peace. You can call it equilibrium. You can call it adjustment, but, essentially, it is relaxation. And if somebody wants to restore relaxation or acquire relaxation, he has to do one thing and that is to banish fear and anger from his system as much as can be done." (MFMA, p. 222)

"It is good to know what temper means. And…let me tell you it means many things, but one thing I wish to discuss today, particularly. Temper is an act-an act. You speak in temper; you distort your features, and all of these are acts. You perhaps move your arms. You flash your eyes. You perhaps blanche or get red in the face. All of these are acts. And an act has this characteristic, that it begins with an intention." (MFMA, p. 244)

"The patient, after relieving the impulse, the temperamental impulse, actually has a brief moment of relief. He got something off his chest. But in the next brief moment, somebody reminds him that now the honeymoon is over. What happens then? Then the patient now is provoked himself. First he provoked the listener. Now he is provoked because he is answered in temper or is condemned or laughed at. And now he had a moment of relief, and he craves that moment back. So the only way to get relief in such a situation is to release another volley of temper, and then he has again relief until the other fellow steps in and the relief is gone." (MFMA, p. 169)

"There would be very little nervous confusion and nervous trouble and very few nervous symptoms, if there were no temper." (MFMA, p. 244)

"If you begin a temperamental argument, that means you declare somebody being wrong or having done wrong to you. And...what you want to do if you don't use violence is to convince your partner that he is wrong and to make him mend his ways." (MFMA, p. 245)

"If you declare something ridiculous-your own reaction-if you declare it as ridiculous, then you don't take it seriously. And there is never an anger that is not taken seriously." (MFMA, p. 293)

"It is good to know what temper means. And...let me tell you it means many things, but one thing I wish to discuss today, particularly. Temper is an act-an act. You speak in temper; you distort your features, and all of these are acts. You perhaps move your arms. You flash your eyes. You perhaps blanche or get red in the face. All of these are acts. And an act has this characteristic, that it begins with an intention." (MFMA, p. 244)

"After a temperamental outburst, there are only casualties, only casualties. You are exhausted, and the other fellow is exhausted. There are casualties, a battlefield strewn with casualties. In most instances, only two casualties; sometimes more, especially if nations become temperamental and start war. Accomplished is usually nothing, but casualties are many." (MFMA, p. 246)

TENSENESS

"Any distrust that you create within you against somebody else, but more so against yourself, will create tenseness. And as long as this self-distrust is maintained, the tenseness will stay with you. It will endure. It will gain duration. And that's the principal characteristic of the nervous patient: that he is likely to produce what other people don't have to produce, and this is enduring tenseness, because he is enduringly disturbed now by his self-distrust." (MFMA, p. 264)

"All the experiences of a nervous patient can be reduced to the fact that he develops tenseness. Without tenseness, the patient would relax, normally relax. He would have average relaxation. But with tenseness, relaxation is gone. And if relaxation is gone and tenseness installs itself on an enduring basis, then symptoms appear." (MFMA, p. 265)

"Tenseness cannot be maintained if you don't fear, or if you are not angry. You must neither be fearful nor angry, and there will be no tenseness, as far as humanly possible." (MFMA, p. 265)

THOUGHTS

"The best means of reducing an idea of danger to its absurdity is to act against it." (MHTWT, p. 366-367)

"Patients without number have assured me that they 'try and try' to get rid of a disturbing idea but 'it just doesn't work.' My standard reply to remarks of this kind is that if I try to shake off an upsetting or ugly thought I invariably fail, no matter how hard I may 'try and try' until I recognize that I don't know how to do it and give up the futile effort. To forget means to let a memory die away, to permit it to drop out of consciousness…the brain knows very well how to do the job of forgetting because it does it continuously." (Selections, p. 73)

"If, as some maintain, sex exercises a powerful influence on average daily existence the effect is due to the *thought about sex* rather than to the sexual impulses as such. Aside from the exceptional instances of sex aberrations and sex delinquencies, sex life in itself is not likely to result in abnormal behavior. It produces maladjustment only or mainly if it is linked to such thoughts as sin, guilt, disgrace, self-blame and self-contempt, expectation of punishment and anticipation of dire consequence to health. Again, you see how even here thought dominates feeling." (P v. P, p. 190)

"I said that feelings lie to you, that they deceive and betray you. How can that be? How can feelings be true or false? If you are sad what has that to do with truth, deception or treachery? Feelings are either experienced or they are not. They are present or absent but never true or false. Thoughts alone possess the quality of truth and falseness. And if the patient's feelings tell lies they do so because an incorrect and deceptive thought is attached to them.

The deception is accomplished by the thought, not by the feeling." (MHTWT, p. 118)

"I...advise you to reject this contemporary superstition that your thoughts are forever scheming against your welfare and your feelings continually plotting against your health." (MHTWT, p. 140)

"My supreme and only duty is to relieve my patients of their agonies. And if their panics and vicious cycles result from their faulty use of the thinking process I shall advise them to throw overboard the rubbish of modern slogans and let me do their thinking in the matter of interpreting and concluding with regard to symptoms." (MHTWT, p. 226)

TOTAL/PARTIAL VIEW

"Everybody who has a head pressure-I have them frequently-does not immediately go into tantrums because it is unbearable. The average person bears a pain, but the patient does not want to... The average person bears a pain, especially a pain that he has had repeatedly in the past, because he is linked to the past and does not particularly consider this day but the total time of his total life. And looking back into his previous life, into this total of his life, he knows that his head pressure has been severe at many times in his history, and it hasn't killed him, and he bore it bravely and patiently, so he bears it again. He is determined to bear it again." (MFMA, p. 104-105)

TRIVIALITIES

"Events in outer environment, and even in inner environment, are routine in the overwhelming majority of instances." (MFMA, p. 108)

"Current psychologies stress the momentous events in life... Momentous events are interesting from the viewpoint of intellectual curiosity but relatively unimportant in the scheme of average adjustment. The average individual adjusts with comparative ease to the great upheavals of life…What taxes the adjustive capacity of the average individual are the more or less continuous, repetitious and habitual irritations of common everyday life." (P v. P, p. 40)

"Whenever you find irreparable rifts and unabridged dissension among close relatives be certain they took their inception, in nine cases out of ten, from…trivial irritations." (P v. P, p. 67)

"The daily round of the average individual consists, in the main, of such trivial performances as reading, conversing, working on a job, cooking, washing, cleaning, telephoning, shopping…In trivial or routine activities, no calamity arises if perchance a mistake occurs. This is the reason why realists, that is, men and women of average aspirations, go about their daily tasks with due caution and circumspection, it is true, but without any marked fear of making a mistake. Mistakes made in trivial performances are trivial themselves, and their possible consequences are just as trivial and not to be feared." (MHTWT, p. 249)

"And if anybody wants to look down his nose on Recovery and say, 'Look here, they talk trivialities,' then I'll agree with him. We talk trivialities, and it is these trivialities which touch on averageness, and it is the principle of averageness that makes you human and healthy. And I will advise you, don't expect that your condition, being as complex as it is – and I don't deny that – requires complex methods to check it and to conquer it. That's not so. The simple method is always the superior procedure." (MFMA, p. 76)

"I have fortunately trained my patients to have respect for intellect and therefore not to think that they are intellectuals. They are average people. Their intellect has not been thoroughly trained as, let me say, as a great scientist's intellect…Let them talk about average trivialities. And whoever wants to talk of something else— of stirring events in politics, in art, in literature--let them listen to other panels. Maybe they are held. I don't know. But don't let them listen to my patients. My patients are obliged by me to speak of nothing but trivialities, that means of life as it pulsates, as it lives, as it is close, and not of artificial issues like politics, economy, and other things that are artificial in the mouth of somebody who has no special knowledge in these fields." (MFMA, p. 141)

"It is the everyday life in which my patients bungle their job of living. They don't bungle it in the political field, not in the economic field, and not in any other field, but daily living. And daily life consists of trivialities." (MFMA, p. 1)

"It's the most astonishing thing, and yet it's common, that people in general think that life-the life of the average individual-is anything but trivialities." (MFMA, p. 261)

"The sense of shame, of fear, of hatred, of contempt applied to trivialities of life have this in common: that they are utterly out of the range of humor. A person hating trivialities, fearing trivialities, being ashamed of daily trivialities, has, of course, no sense of humor. And my patients, as long as they are suffering from their panics, from their frightful sensations and impulses, and so forth, have, of course, no sense of humor. They take their inner experiences too seriously." (MFMA, p. 96-97)

"What you are likely to bungle is not an emergency. An emergency rolls on. Sometimes you can stop it. But if you can't stop it, that's no bungling. That may happen to anybody. That's an average occurrence, that human beings are unequal to emergencies or to catastrophes. But daily life is something that human beings should be adjusted to. They should be able to deal with it satisfactorily." (MFMA, p. 108-109)

"Trivialities of everyday life have one peculiarity: that they either are not noticed because they don't interest you, or they cheer you because they please you, or they anger you or scare you…You see, trivialities crowd the life, but any one of them may arouse your anger, your fear, your disgust, your terror, and so forth." (MFMA, p. 137)

"The closer is a relation between one individual and the other, the more can the trivialities performed by the one person irritate and frustrate and anger and scare the other person if they are a close unit, like mother and baby, or other such associations." (MFMA, p. 137)

"What we call *reality* has a certain corner in which a person sometimes dies, and another person gets married, and a house burns down, and a bankruptcy happens. But in the vast expanse of the remainder of reality, what is called *reality* could just as well be called *triviality*. Reality really consists of trivialities, mainly. But the patient, before he reaches Recovery, doesn't know that. And he doesn't know that his trouble has started as a triviality." (MFMA, p. 262)

"When a nervous patient feels fatigued, then he doesn't say, 'I am tired.' Well, that would be a very trivial statement, and the patient doesn't make trivial statements. The patient complains, and a complaint is very difficult to make about a trivial thing. If the patient complains, then he is prompted to exaggerate. If he doesn't exaggerate, then his complaint is trivial. So, I have yet to see the patients that don't-when they think of their fatigue-that don't express it in terms of exhaustion. Fatigue isn't enough. It is not dramatic enough. It's not impressive enough. And the patient somehow gets himself to believe that he suffers from exhaustion. But I correct him and tell him it's fatigue. He doesn't like that as a rule." (MFMA, p. 271)

VANITY/PRIDE

"If somebody is vain, this means he thinks he knows better than somebody else, he is better than somebody else, he wants the attention of people, he wants to occupy the center of the stage. What does he accomplish there? What is the obstacle? Anybody can be loud and, let me say, display poor manners. All it requires is to have an impulse to do it and follow it through. There is no obstacle to poor manners if you wish to display them. And if then you are proud because you have called attention to yourself, that's not pride. That's vanity. You call it pride, perhaps, but it is vanity." (MFMA, p. 198)

"In pride, you exercise strength. In vanity, you try to exercise force. In pride, you try to exercise strength over your inner impulses, sensations, feelings. That is self-control. In vanity, you try to attract the attention of others. You try to exercise power over others. You try to push them aside and push you forward. That's the exercise of force, not of strength, and certainly not strength of character." (MFMA, p. 199)

VICIOUS/VITALIZING CYCLE

"My supreme and only duty is to relieve my patients of their agonies. And if their panics and vicious cycles result from their faulty use of the thinking process I shall advise them to throw overboard the rubbish of modern slogans and let me do their thinking in the matter of interpreting and concluding with regard to symptoms." (MHTWT, p. 226)

Dr. Low to a patient: "Once you commanded your speech muscles to move the very action of the muscles had a vitalizing effect on the brain. The movement of the muscles convinced the brain that speaking is possible. And when the brain witnessed the living, vital performance of the muscles it acquired a new vitality itself and lost its lifelessness. The more forceful was the action of the muscles the more vitalized became the brain; the more vital the brain the more forceful the muscles. By commanding your muscles to move you had thus transformed the *vicious cycle of helplessness* into the *vitalizing cycle of self-confidence*." (MHTWT, p. 374)

"If muscles get two contradictory orders at the same time, all they can do is to create tenseness or to begin to tremble or to stiffen up or all three together. And then there is no action. And you will understand that the patient can in this manner confuse the muscles, irritate them, throwing them into tenseness and spasms and in tremors. This means making them react like you react in temper: tenseness, stiffness. And that's what the muscles do, and then there is no leadership. The person doesn't exercise guidance, doesn't give guidance. And if this happens, the person notices that the muscles don't do as he wants them to do, so he now becomes more irritated, more suspicious that there may be something wrong with him, and therefore more temperamental. And a vicious cycle develops." (MFMA, p. 117)

VICTIMIZATION

"Once you think of yourself as being a victim, you will not try to seek help from your inner environment, from yourself." (MFMA, p. 49-50)

WANTS VS. NEEDS

"The patient must get to know what is a need, and that must be supplied; and what is merely a want, and that may be supplied. It may be legitimate to supply it, but not when it clashes with a need." (MFMA, p. 284)

"Peace is the food of life, a value and objective need while excitement is merely the spice and thrill of life, a desirability (not a value) and nothing but a subjective want." (MHTWT, p. 200)

"A person's reasoning is powerfully influenced by the values cultivated in his group. And our contemporary group has placed a preposterous valuation on romanto-intellectual wants to the detriment of realistic needs." (MHTWT, p. 202)

"It takes effort to wait if you suffer. It takes effort even to wait for an elevator, even if you don't suffer. To wait for a streetcar, that is effort. It certainly is not comfort, you know that. And what the patient wants-again I go back to the theme-is comfort. But that's not precisely what he needs. It is only what he wants" (MFMA, p. 273)

"The group wants you to do what you need, not what you want... the group has one goal, and the individual has another goal. The group is not in the way of the individual, but it's not interested in it. If you want to take a swim, the group is not against it, but the group is definitely against it if you want to take a swim while some task waits to be performed. The group wants you to discharge your obligations. But the individual, when he is in trouble, has inclinations, the inclination to get relief." (MFMA, p. 274)

"It may surprise you, but it is a truth, that my system of training patients is mainly based on the distinction between needs, which are objective, and wants, which are purely subjective." (MFMA, p. 285)

"The patient is eager to express his wants, mainly. He is not so eager to pursue his needs. His need is health, nothing else, aside from what I mentioned, necessities of existence. But his supreme need is health, and you will not deny that. But that's not what he wants. He merely wishes it." (MFMA, p. 285)

"If I have now the impulse, or the wish, or desire to ask for help, then I naturally want to get this help immediately, right now, if I suffer severely. And that's what we call the short-range goal. The goal that is now in the patient's mind is meant to bring something on this minute. It's a momentary, short-range goal...My goal that I set before the patient is not meant to get into action or to be reached this moment. It is meant to be reached in weeks or months. So the goal that I have set for the patient is a long-range goal. But the patient who suffers now is not particularly interested in what is going to happen in five, six, or ten months. He wants relief now and not a minute later. And you will now understand that that's what the patient wants. That's his want but the goal that I set for him is his need." (MFMA, p. 286)

"The patient, in my opinion, is little interested in what he needs, and all interested in what he wants. And the result is that the patient who constantly hunts for attention, who tries to force those around him to offer the attention, this patient, with his constant drive for affection, attention and sympathy, alienates those around him...He himself blocks his path toward reaching the goal that he needs to reach, because he alienates everybody around him. And the poor wretch cannot help it. He is driven by an overpowering impulse to do it, to do that thing that neither brings fulfillment for what he wants, nor for what he needs." (MFMA, p. 287)

WILL

"The Will has one function only: it rejects or accepts ideas, and stops or releases impulses." (MHTWT, p. 136)

"You may have difficulty controlling fears and worries. But muscles can be controlled 'at will.' Everybody has it within his power to command his muscles to effect an act or to refrain from effecting it." (MHTWT, p. 350)

"The problem adult has good insight into his missteps both outside and inside the home but makes use of it in one of the spheres only. In his outside contacts he *chooses* to exercise his insight; in his domestic contacts he *chooses* not to exercise it." (P v. P, p. 89)

"At the risk of being intolerably monotonous and repetitious I shall recite the well-known fact that temperamental persons, as a rule, display their tempers solely or mainly with the members of their immediate family and with their employees. In the company of strangers and friends, and particularly in the presence of 'important' people, like superiors, hosts and hostesses, their nature is pleasingly tamed, their instinct neatly controlled and their heredity conveniently forgotten. Most of it is clearly not inborn but acquired." (P v. P, p. 100)

"Get it into your heads that a human being has the power to choose what to believe and what not to believe. This power to choose is called the Will." (MHTWT, p. 141)

"Beliefs are frequently stubborn and obstinate...Muscles are just as likely to develop obstinacy. They tend to acquire set patterns of behavior preferring certain well grooved acts and avoiding others. Just think of the habits of procrastination, of twitches and spasms, of restlessness and sluggishness, and you will realize that muscles are not always pliant tools in the hands of the Will. In order to pry loose the resisting beliefs and rebellious muscles attempt after attempt must be made to dislodge them from their comfortable berth and to force them to give up resistance. The resistance may be so strong that the attempts to break it must be repeated in innumerable trials before success is achieved. This requires the Will to use a great deal of power in continued strenuous practice." (MHTWT, p. 141-142)

"My patients will have to realize what former generations always knew: that a life task can be mastered only through a grueling, exacting learning process in which all the resources of the Will must combine to achieve final fulfillment. Health is a task of this kind. It can be secured only if the patient's Will initiates a system of ceaseless trials and trials and trials until in the end the task is accomplished. If this is done even the most stubborn belief will yield to the influence of the learning process and the most sluggish muscle will obey the dictates of the Will." (MHTWT, p. 144)

"If a person is seized with grief or stimulated by joy it would be senseless for the Will to claim that the joy is false or the grief impossible. Feelings are either experienced or not experienced. Their existence, wisdom and probability cannot be denied or affirmed. The same holds for sensations. If the head aches it would be absurd for the Will to object that, 'No, this is no headache. It is unwise, untrue or improbable.' Clearly, if the Will is to intervene in order to control the total experience of insecurity its 'no' cannot be directed to feelings and sensations. Instead, it must address itself to thoughts and impulses." (MHTWT, p. 137)

"We in Recovery will have nothing of a theory which relegates life, more particularly life in a group, to blind instincts and capricious drives. We have solidly embraced a viewpoint which considers action as based or capable of being based on deliberate plans and settled decisions, on reasoned conclusions and firm determinations. And plans, decisions, conclusions and determinations are guided by the Will; they are not or do not have to be driven by instincts. (MHTWT, p. 194)

"With the spread of specialism, self-help and self-management have ceased to play a significant part in the present-day domestic, marital and social scene. The habit of rushing to the expert for advice has resulted in a vicious cycle of helplessness: the more the expert's aid is solicited the more helpless is the applicant bound to feel; the greater the helplessness the more urgent the need for further consultations; the more frequent the consultations the more poignant the sense of helplessness. In the end, an individual emerges who has a stunted Will, a meager 'know-how', and a famished sense of resourcefulness, in short, Modern Man, the pathetic creature of an extraneous Will, without plans or directions of his own and in abject dependence on forces outside his inner self." (MHTWT, p. 143-144)

"In Recovery, you are taught to approach the business of getting well in the spirit of performing a task and meaning business. The business calls, first and foremost, for labor and exertion and self-control, in other words, for the Will to Effort." (MHTWT, p. 219)

"I do not presume to know whether physical nature can be changed… but what I know for certain is that human nature, that is, human dispositions, can be changed at will and with ease whenever it is convenient, desirable or mandatory." (MHTWT, p. 255)

"Everybody who has a head pressure-I have them frequently-does not immediately go into tantrums because it is unbearable. The average person bears a pain, but the patient does not want to… The average person bears a pain, especially a pain that he has had repeatedly in the past, because he is linked to the past and does not particularly consider this day but the total time of his total life. And looking back into his previous life, into this total of his life, he knows that his head pressure has been severe at many times in his history, and it hasn't killed him, and he bore it bravely and patiently, so he bears it again. He is determined to bear it again." (MFMA, p. 104-105)

"An average person can have fears and go ahead and act his life regardless of the fear. And that's what you are trained to do in Recovery. In Recovery, we tell you everything that you suffer from – fears, angers, anxieties, pains, pressures – it's all average. And all of these are happenings, accidents, chance events. But now you must exercise something that is not chance but choice, not accident but intention, and that is the will. Have the will to go through your fears and angers and pressures like an average person does or is expected to do. And if you do that, then you will have carried out the main principle of the training which we give here, and, in addition, you will get well." (MFMA, p. 160)

"When I go out on the street and it is raining, I didn't make the rain. The rain has nothing to do with my will. That happens. But there is something else in this matter of the rain. I could have done something about it. I could have provided myself with a raincoat, with an umbrella. I could have listened to the radio and could, perhaps, have known whether it would be raining, and then I could have done something about it. I might have stayed home if I could. You see, this is no longer a happening. This is dependent on whether I exercise my will. To take precautions against the happening means to have the will to be cautious. And that's a will. A will…is something that chooses. I could go out in the rain, and I could stay home, and I have to choose between these two possibilities. So, will is the same thing as choice." (MFMA, p. 157-158)

WILL TO BEAR DISCOMFORT

"Nervous patients are convinced that what they fear are certain acts or certain occurrences while, in point of fact, the only fear they experience is that of a discomfort which they conceive of as 'unendurable' or 'intolerable' or 'unbearable'. To put it bluntly: nervous fear is the fear of discomfort." (MHTWT, p. 146)

"If you want to maintain the values of health and self-respect, of initiative and determination, of character and self-discipline, what you will have to learn is to bear the discomfort of controlling your impulses, of steeling your Will, of curbing your temper. This calls for an attitude which far from exalting the virtues of comfort places the emphasis where it belongs: on THE WILL TO BEAR DISCOMFORT." (MHTWT, p. 149)

"Those of my patients who are slow in improving suffer from a dual, divided Will. They want to get well but want it to come to them painlessly, without painful practice. They want health, but they do not want the discomfort of practicing rules and techniques. This means that they want and do not want." (Selections, p. 96)

"Many things in a nervous patient are depressed and crowded out of the stream of life. They are in life but don't 'stream.' And in order to make the stream flow again, the stream of feeling, the stream of interest, the stream of mental reaction and emotional reaction, what is required is for the patient not to discourage himself. And in order not to discourage himself, the patient must be trained, trained to develop courage, trained to develop the capacity for braving discomfort-even if you call it torture, but it's still discomfort. And once you learn that, after due training, there is no difficulty to have both validity and vitality restored to its former function, which is then as lively as it ever was." (MFMA, p. 68-69)

"When you have palpitations, it's very easy and no effort whatever to run to the phone and call the doctor. That's easy. That's comfort, or the prospect of comfort. Here in this organization you are trained to stand discomfort and to make a strenuous effort. And a supreme effort for a nervous patient is to stand his symptoms, not to run to the phone to call the physician, and it's remarkable what you do when you decide to stand the discomfort of the symptom." (MFMA, p. 5)

"I have seen patients who reported to me that once they made up their minds, this means they made the decision to stand the torture of any kind of symptom, the symptom was gone, in many cases in an instant. So you have the choice between effort, particularly the effort of the decision, and the comfort of running for help-that's comfort-either to the doctor or somewhere else. And while you're running for help, you must tell the story, and while telling the story, you work yourself up and become temperamental and emotional, and that makes the symptom worse. If you shun the effort of standing your discomfort, you are in trouble. If you make the decision to stand it, then you may dispose of your symptom in a fraction of a second, or at some longer interval." (MFMA, p. 5-6)

"This organization does not stand for any kind of particular philosophy, except that it emphasizes what is called *common sense*. But it stands for effort and for the principle-well, the principle I guess-to have the will to bear discomfort, which I will now change and give it another phrasing, and you should have the will to stand torture. This is the road to health if the tolerance of torture is gained through persistent training." (MFMA, p. 6)

"Everybody who has a head pressure-I have them frequently-does not immediately go into tantrums because it is unbearable. The average person bears a pain, but the patient does not want to… The average person bears a pain, especially a pain that he has had repeatedly in the past, because he is linked to the past and does not particularly consider this day but the total time of his total life. And looking back into his previous life, into this total of his life, he knows that his head pressure has been severe at many times in his history, and it hasn't killed him, and he bore it bravely and patiently, so he bears it again. He is determined to bear it again." (MFMA, p. 104-105)

"It takes effort to wait if you suffer. It takes effort even to wait for an elevator, even if you don't suffer. To wait for a streetcar, that is effort. It certainly is not comfort, you know that. And what the patient wants-again I go back to the theme-is comfort. But that's not precisely what he needs. It is only what he wants" (MFMA, p. 273)

"It's difficult to know what comfort is permissible and what effort is dispensable. And when the patient, for instance, wants some comfort, why shouldn't he get it? And he should get it if it can be provided. But if it interferes with a duty and obligation, for instance, the duty to get well, then I would advise the patient not to look for comfort and rather to make an effort to reach the goal of health." (MFMA, p. 274)

WILL VS. FATE

"You are not responsible, first, for the fact that you have weak nerves. Second, you are not responsible for the fact that somebody else gets well more quickly than you do. Nobody will be fair if he holds that against you, because there are so-called individual differences...for which fate is responsible and not you and your will." (MFMA, p. 14)

"When I have an impulse, be certain I did not summon it. I did not call it into being. I didn't make any effort to get this impulse started, especially if it is an impulse that I hate, that I don't want. Then be certain I am not responsible for it. This means I didn't create it. I didn't do anything to bring it to the fore. So why should I blame myself? Why should I feel disgraced?...And...that's what all of you do." (MFMA, p. 450)

"Organic disturbances, that is, complications created by Fate, act indiscriminately and without selection. They may strike any person at any time in any place. Once they have struck they do not pick out shrewdly certain occasions in which they will make a stage appearance or certain others in which they will keep cunningly off the stage. If a symptom is regularly present in one set of conditions and regularly absent in another, the judicious choice cannot be the result of Fate which is never selective. It must be the outflow of Will whose very function is to choose and select." (Selections, p. 60)

"We in Recovery will have nothing of a theory which relegates life, more particularly life in a group, to blind instincts and capricious drives. We have solidly embraced a viewpoint which considers action as based or capable of being based on deliberate plans and settled decisions, on reasoned conclusions and firm determinations. And plans, decisions, conclusions and determinations are guided by the Will; they are not or do not have to be driven by instincts." (MHTWT, p. 194)

"It [the impulse] always comes by Fate. I get such impulses, much more dreadful impulses. But my nerves have been steeled and trained to develop resistance, and when dreadful and mischievous and lascivious and blasphemous impulses reach my brain, I look away and wait and they will depart. And they depart in no time because my resistance has been strengthened and Fate is not strong enough to break my resistance once it is strengthened through training." (MDO, p. 144)

"It is true that I can stub my toe against a sharp edge, and that may be fate, but it may be something else. It may be that I was negligent, careless. It may be that if I had exercised my will, I would have paid proper attention to things around me, and I would have avoided kicking against the sharp edge. You will now understand one and the same accident that happens, or event that happens, may be due to fate, but it may also be due to a lagging will, to the will that lags in the matter of attention. And it will be good for you to know that these are the main forces in this world. We call them *fate*, which is thoroughly impersonal, and *will*, which is thoroughly personal." (MFMA, p. 12)

"Now let me tell you, when you develop a poor resistance in your nervous system, whether you develop it or whether it is born with you does not matter, but if you have a poor resistance, that was done by fate. You simply don't know yourself, how to arrange it that you create a poor resistance...You did not want to have poor resistance, by no means. And so all of you, when you had your first symptoms, or your first break, or your first decline in nervous reactions, you had it as a heritage from fate. You were not responsible for what happened to you." (MFMA, p. 12-13)

"You are not responsible for your nervous reactions, and you are not responsible for handling them properly or improperly as long as nobody has shown you how they can be handled properly. But once somebody has shown you how you can handle your nervous system so that it gets a bigger share of resistance, and you don't apply what you have been given in technique and training, then-and now the symptoms get worse, or when the symptoms don't get measurable better-then you are responsible." (MFMA, p. 13)

"Our method is built on the principle that in minor complications like nervous symptoms-even if they are severe they are only minor complications-in minor complications you must set your will against fate, and once you set your will against fate, you relax, and nature has then an opportunity to correct the complication because our body, this means nature, is a self-repairing machine." (MFMA, p. 17)

"When I go out on the street and it is raining, I didn't make the rain. The rain has nothing to do with my will. That happens. But there is something else in this matter of the rain. I could have done something about it. I could have provided myself with a raincoat, with an umbrella. I could have listened to the radio and could, perhaps, have known whether it would be raining, and then I could have done something about it. I might have stayed home if I could. You see, this is no longer a happening. This is dependent on whether I exercise my will. To take precautions against the happening means to have the will to be cautious. And that's a will. A will...is something that chooses. I could go out in the rain, and I could stay home, and I have to choose between these two possibilities. So, will is the same thing as choice." (MFMA, p. 157-158)

NOTES

NOTES